John Oldcastle

Memorials of Cardinal Manning

John Oldcastle

Memorials of Cardinal Manning

ISBN/EAN: 9783743346574

Manufactured in Europe, USA, Canada, Australia, Japa

Cover: Foto ©Lupo / pixelio.de

Manufactured and distributed by brebook publishing software (www.brebook.com)

John Oldcastle

Memorials of Cardinal Manning

Fac-simile of an article written by Cardinal Manning for "The Weekly Register."

MEMORIALS OF
Cardinal Manning

From Barraud's Photograph.

ARRANGED AND EDITED BY
JOHN OLDCASTLE

LONDON: BURNS & OATES, LTD.
NEW YORK: CATHOLIC PUBLICATION SOCIETY.

Dedication.

TO THE MOTHER-GENERAL

AND TO THE COMMUNITY

AT NAZARETH HOUSE, HAMMERSMITH,

WHO LAID

THE FIRST WREATH UPON HIS GRAVE,

THESE FIRST MEMORIALS OF CARDINAL MANNING

ARE INSCRIBED.

To meet a wide demand, these Memorials, originally prepared for a Magazine, are now issued in a more permanent form.

The Editor heartily thanks the correspondents who have so kindly favoured him with Letters and Reminiscences for publication in these Memorials.

"MERRY ENGLAND" Office,
    43, Essex Street, Strand

MEMORIALS OF CARDINAL MANNING.

THE LIFE AT LAVINGTON.

HENRY EDWARD MANNING was twenty-six years of age when he went from Oxford to Lavington. He took with him to this Sussex village, situated amid lovely downs, the reputation of a brilliant career at the University. Perhaps the Sussex villagers who formed his first congregation of a dozen or twenty at the little outlying hamlet at Upwaltham did not care much for such antecedents. Possibly they did not lay great stress on appearances either, and were unaware that the curate was rated by Mr. Gladstone as one of the three handsomest men of his time. But both the glory of his career and the spiritual beauty of his countenance were likely to be observed by the family of the patron of the living, Mr. John Sargent, the old Squire of Lavington. He had then an elderly son, the Rev. John Sargent, who held the family living, and who had four fair. daughters. It was as their father's curate that Manning began his life at Lavington. The four daughters of his Rector made a remarkable group. They had been to Oxford more than once to see a brother, and Manning met them there. " In 1829," says the Rev. Thomas Mozley, " I met all the four celebrated sisters together at breakfast at Robert Wilberforce's, and looked at them with a strong mixture of curiosity and admiration." Talking them over the next day with Henry Wilberforce, Mozley chanced to say that he admired Mary's "cool" expression and manner—a

The Life at Lavington.

phrase which he was reminded of for fifty years. The eldest of the four girls—Emily—married Samuel Wilberforce, afterwards Bishop of Oxford. Mary, the second girl, to whose calmness and recollection Mozley had given the dubious epithet, became Mrs. Henry Wilberforce. The third daughter, Caroline, lives in the memory of a few as Mrs. Henry Edward Manning, and the youngest—Sophia—("a very sylph in form and feature") married the Rev. George Dudley Ryder. The four girls had a brother—Henry. "I met him," writes Mr. Mozley, "at a Common-room breakfast at Oriel, the day of his matriculation. His life was watched by many who had heard the old saying, that no heir to the Lavington estate had ever succeeded his own father. He seemed to me in health and strength. I did, indeed, see the peach-blossom in his cheeks, but saw no harm in it. A fortnight after that he was gone." The Squire of Lavington, losing thus his only grandson in the male line, was also to lose his only son, so that the Rectory was left empty of its natural occupant as well as of its natural heir. Thus it was that when the Rev. John Sargent died in 1833, aged fifty-three, his curate of only a few months' standing was presented by the Squire, who survived his son and his grandson, to the livings of Lavington and Graffham. It was seven months later, on the 7th of November, 1833, that the new Rector married the granddaughter of his patron. There, in the Rectory, sheltered by the Downs and covered with roses nearly throughout the year, Manning passed what he always remembered as the happiest years of his life. His study is well remembered by his nephew, the present Squire of Lavington, as "a long room with a southern aspect, the walls covered from ceiling to floor with books, the high desk where Manning stood, not sat, to write."* A very

---

* Mr. Reginald Wilberforce has placed readers under a deep obligation by his article on "Cardinal Manning in the Church of England" (*Nineteenth Century*, February, 1892), which contains, besides most interesting personal reminiscences, a full account of certain aspects of the Anglican life of the Archdeacon which can be only glanced at here.

The Life at Lavington.

different look-out, over a piece of waste land, with a vista of stores and workman's dwellings, belonged to the library of his future home—Archbishop's House, Westminster. That was not, however, the room in which he read and wrote, though he would come from his own inner room to be photographed there, as he is seen in a portrait we print; and in that room, too, he received many visitors who will recognise the now empty chair in which they were wont to see him, and which is the subject of another illustration. In the Lavington library the young Rector read the *Record* week by week; and the "Tracts for the Times." The *Record* began to hold him less, the "Tracts" to hold him more; and by steady degrees he assimilated the great doctrines which in seven years led him to give up Lavington and to join the Catholic Church. It is true that "Tract XC." mystified and even vexed him. He thought its special pleading was less than English in outspoken honesty. It was in that library, with the late roses trellising the windows, that Gladstone, the rising hope of the State, sat with Manning, the rising hope of the Church,* when the secession of Newman had come on the one and the other like a blow. True, the Churchman made haste to comfort himself with the reflection that the dangers of "one man leadership," and of a clique taking the place of the community, had been eased or ended by this apparent catastrophe (it was really absolute continuity) in the "Newmania" at Oxford. He was taking other aids to himself, which in after years must have struck him as more shadowy still. So when Mr. Gladstone asked: "Are all these conversions to be regarded as separate testimonies to the truth of Rome, or can they all be explained away by some common defect?" the Archdeacon (he was a very young Archdeacon) replied: "They can be so explained. There is one defect undermining the character of the seceders—

---

* Bishop Philpotts..."Henry of Exeter"—used to say at this time that there were three men to whom the country had mainly to look: Manning in the Church, Gladstone in the State, and Hope-Scott in the Law.

want of truth." The memory of "Tract XC." still worked in his mind; but his own subsequent conduct was to afford the most practically complete retractation of the judgment too hastily expressed.

THE UNRESTING RECTOR AND ARCHDEACON.

Among his other clerical activities the unresting Manning pulled down and rebuilt both the churches at Lavington and Graffham. The church at Lavington is still the same as Manning left it; carrying on its eastern front a large flint, set there by his own hands. The font was a present from his dear friend, destined to be his fellow-convert, Mr. Hope-Scott, Q.C. Graffham Church was less successful, for it was too dark on dull days to be without candles. "See how an Archdeacon with the best intentions can spoil a church," he used to say when he showed it to his friends. It has been since rebuilt as a personal memorial to his brother-in-law, Bishop Samuel Wilberforce. Manning's habit was to robe in the Rectory, and walk the short distance to the church for both morning and evening prayer in full canonicals; and his beautiful figure is still a local tradition. When, as a Cardinal, he visited the re-built church, his nephew, Mr. Reginald Wilberforce, showed him a New Testament, with the inscription "H. E. Manning, 1845." He laid his hand on the book, saying, "Times change and men change; but this never changes." As Rector he was beloved in his parish, his nephew bears witness. "One of his old parishioners still rejoices in the fact that for some years she led the singing in Lavington Church, 'saving his poor voice, and giving it a rest, dear man.' To the children he was invariably kind, constantly giving them small money presents. It is told of him that when he saw a child with bad boots on, he used to say: 'Now, my child, I will give you one new boot if your mother can afford to buy you the other'; then he went to the village shop and paid for one boot for the

The Grapple with Grief.

child." When the Cardinal died, some of those old boys of his at Lavington had their rugged faces "wet with tears of genuine love and sorrow, while many a younger man, who knew him only by tradition, asked, 'Is it true that *the Archdeacon* is dead?'"

THE HUSBAND.

But it must be with the domestic life of the future Cardinal that Lavington Rectory is most intimately associated. The marriage with Caroline Sargent, at which Samuel Wilberforce officiated, on the 7th of November in 1833, resulted in an ideally happy companionship, closed by death at the end of a little more than three years and a-half. "I have a vision of his lovely wife which I shall never forget," writes Lord Coleridge, whom the Cardinal knew from the time when the future Lord Chief Justice was a boy, and whose career he watched with affectionate pride. "Many still remember," Mr. Reginald Wilberforce writes, "his young wife, with beautiful eyes and the characteristic fairness of the Sargent family." What a large part his experiences of happy married life had in the formation of his character, and how it showed itself in his wise and tender relations with women, all must be aware who were intimate with the Cardinal Archbishop.

THE GRAPPLE WITH GRIEF.

And the impression made upon Henry Edward Manning by the loss which befell him in 1837 was equally marked. It is best told in Mr. Reginald Wilberforce's words: "That the early death of his beautiful wife deeply affected a character like Manning's is not to be wondered at; but it did more than transiently affect him, it set a seal on his character that was never afterwards effaced. After her death he found himself unable to dwell on the past except in direct acts of devotion: 'At those times, in church, but specially day by day

The Grapple with Grief.

at home, I both can and do fully and fixedly, and they are the most blessed moments of my present life. At all other times I feel the absolute need of full employment, and to the best of my power I maintain a habit of fixed attention, and suffer as few intervals of disengaged time as I can.'" There was the secret of that rigid restraint and that fixity of purpose which marked him out henceforth from all other men. To the end of his life, the 24th of July was a day when he religiously kept the memory of the beloved dead. At the time of her death he recorded what he describes as "a sort of grapple with what was crushing me"—persuasions against grief, how powerful yet poor!

Had you not rather bear yourself all the affliction of anxiety and grief which clouds a season of death? The hopes, fears, blights, faintings, and recoils of cold blood on the overwhelmed heart? The quick step, sudden message, hasty summons, the agony of lingering expectation. Somebody must bear this, for it is appointed unto all men once to die, and you must die too at the last. Would you not that they should be spared all you suffer?

Is the solitude of bereavement afflicting?

Would you not rather endure it and let them enter into the fellowship of Saints and Angels? The heavy days, long evenings, leisure changed into loneliness. The sad nights, and sadder days, when the reality of our bereavement breaks in upon us. Sleep, much more dreaming, puts us back where we were, but waking thrusts us again into the present.

Is death terrible, and its avenues rough?

Will you not rejoice for them that they have got their trial well over, and that now there remains for them no more suffering and sickness, because no more sin; that the spirit is now enfranchised, the body laid up for renewal. They shall be restored, not with the hollow eye and sharp severe cries of distress, but in a transfigured perfection of all they once were. Death has dominion only while we are dying. They are born to a new life when the spirit passes forth.

Is it blessed to enter into rest?

Then do you not rejoice that they have entered—aye, so soon? Would you not give way to them, and yield any lesser blessing to them? And will you not rejoice that they have entered into the greatest at the cost of your sorrow and soli-

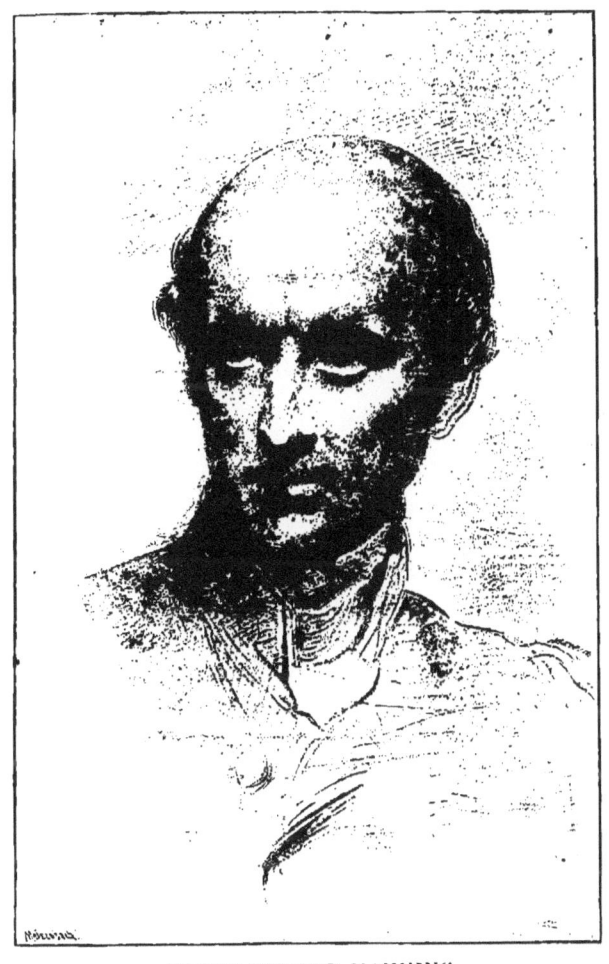

HENRY EDWARD MANNING,
RECTOR OF LAVINGTON AND ARCHDEACON OF CHICHESTER.
(*After the Portrait by George Richmond, R.A.*)

tude? This is only the greatest act of self-denial you have ever been called to for their sakes.

THE WIDOWER.

To her mother Mrs. Manning said on her death-bed, " I am sure you will do all you can to take care of Henry." Mrs. Sargent therefore took up her abode with her widower son-in-law. On the second anniversary of her daughter's death she wrote to another daughter, Mrs. Samuel Wilberforce (soon to follow to the grave):

This has been a week of much painful feeling to dear Henry, and he has wished to spend it exclusively in religious exercises and in his parish. On Wednesday we went soon after breakfast to the shepherd, and dearest H—— administered the Sacrament to him and Mrs. Graysmark, and Mrs. Reeves, and me. He then shut himself up in his room, and after some hours he called me to give me a few memorials for which I had once asked. He was quite in an agony of tears, and only in the evening appeared in the calmest state of mind, and we had service in the church as it was the Eve of St. James. Yesterday we had two services : in the morning here, evening at Graffham, and two nice little lectures. As we were going into this church, Henry said, "My dear friend Gladstone is just now going to be married"; and upon my saying something of the strange differences in the lot of those we love, he said, in the most plaintive voice, "Yes, but it all leads to the same blessed end."

The link between him and Lavington he felt was forged for ever. In 1838 he wrote : " Till the last six months I have never known what it is to have *irresistible* local affection. Once a little self-denial would make all places alike ; for all that makes one place differ from another would have followed me like a shadow. Now there is only one place unlike all others, and therefore unchangeable." Once, when in after years duty brought him into the neighbourhood of Lavington, his first visit was to the little churchyard, where he remained in silence for many minutes by his wife's grave. No stone is placed upon it ; nor does any inscription appear on the window in Chichester Cathedral which records her memory and the love borne to it by him who survived her for more than half-a-century.

DEVELOPMENT.

Archdeacon Manning's belief in the Catholic Church as a visible and teaching body, guided by the Holy Ghost gained in strength as the years at Lavington passed away. Proportionately did the Anglican Establishment as a branch of that Catholic Church lose his allegiance. The Gorham Case came as a crisis. An Anglican clergyman could hold that baptism was a mere empty form, and a secular court upheld him in his benefice. Would the Establishment rise to purge itself of that decision? If not, how could it claim to be an infallible witness to truth? A meeting of earnest Anglicans was held in Mr. Hope-Scott's house in Curzon Street, and a protest was drawn up which Archdeacon Manning was the first to sign. Mr. Gladstone, who stood and warmed himself by the fire, was the first layman who was asked to sign. But he refused. The Archdeacon took him aside. "How can I, consistently with my oath as a Privy Councillor?" he asked. The Archdeacon then announced that Mr. Gladstone's reason for refusal affected no one but himself, and passed to the next name. Father Morris, who says that the Archdeacon believed then as always in "Mr. Gladstone's perfect sincerity and complete good faith of many years," adds the following anecdote:

The quiet state of Mr. Gladstone's conscience is illustrated by a story the Cardinal told me of the moment when his own mind was made up to submit to the Church. Mr. Manning had left his Archdeaconry and had come to London, where, as the guest of his sister in South Audley Street, he spent much time in deliberation and prayer before becoming a Catholic. It is one thing to lose faith in the Church of England; it is another thing, against the prejudices of a life, to arrive at the belief that the Roman Catholic Church, of which the Pope is the visible Head,

Last Words as an Anglican.

is the one true Church of Christ upon earth. This belief was slowly maturing in his mind and heart. One Sunday Mr. Manning and Mr. Gladstone were out walking together, and they dropped into a proprietary chapel in Palace Street, close to the Buckingham Palace stables. The preacher was the Rev. Thomas Harper, who afterwards as a Jesuit Father wrote a reply to Pusey's "Eirenicon" and also an elaborate work called "The Metaphysics of the Schools." His sermon ended with a series of the solemn texts in which Our Lord bids men leave all things to follow Him. "He that loveth father or mother more than Me, is not worthy of Me." "Unless a man renounce all that he possesses, he cannot be My disciple." "If any man would come after Me, let him take up his cross daily and follow Me."—"Does all that say anything to you?" This was the question that Mr. Manning put to Mr. Gladstone when they had left the chapel. "No, I cannot say it does," was Mr. Gladstone's answer. "Well, then, it does to me," said Mr. Manning, "and I am going to act upon it at once."

LAST WORDS AS AN ANGLICAN.

On the 11th of December, 1850—three months before his reception into the Church—Archdeacon Manning dated from 44, Cadogan Place, where he was staying with his sister, a letter to Hope-Scott, in which he said: "It is either Rome or license of thought and will." This letter is well known to readers of the already published collection of His Eminence's letters. It may here be supplemented by a letter written from the same address on the very next day, to an Evangelical clergyman who wrote to dissuade him from leaving the Anglican Church, and who asked him to confer with Richard Waldo Sibthorp—then temporarily halting between two opinions. The Rev. Lord Forrester himself publishes the Archdeacon's reply:

44, Cadogan Place, December 12th, 1850.

MY DEAR BROTHER IN CHRIST,

I put private on this letter that I may write with no restraint, and that what I write may be held by you

Last Words as an Anglican.

as sacred in the charity which unites us, who have never met except before the Throne of Grace. First, let me say I am sorry to be so slow in returning the enclosed letters; they are to me most instructive, and draw me as much to the writer as they warn me from the path in which he outwardly is walking. Would to God I could walk with him in the inward path where his feet tread surely. Also let me thank you for the enclosed hymn, which is beautiful and soothing. I am thankful that you do not find more in my notes on baptism to dissent from, and still more that you hold the great law that the substance and reason of Holy Scripture is the true and Divine source of doctrine. It seems to me that even here "the letter killeth." I have often thought that Holy Scripture is like a crystal in the solar light, perfectly transparent and suffused, luminous and radiant, and yet neither the source of light, nor possessing it, except in the Light. This Light I believe to be the presence of Christ in the Spirit, dwelling in His mystical Body, and the illumination of Faith in which alone Scripture can be read aright. You asked me once how I should answer the question, How can a man be just with God? My faith would answer, by the indwelling of Christ. And now let me thank you for your kind words towards myself. I do indeed believe that, far apart as we seem, we are more deeply in communion than many who are intellectually agreed. Your heart's desires and mine are, I trust, the same: to love and to preach the Lord Jesus. May my few words and poor endeavours be given to Him alone. I know of nothing on this side the grave that has any fairness and sweetness besides this. It is true that I have been in trials, and, after long and painful deliberation, I felt that I could not preserve the integrity of my conscience without resigning what I hold. It has been a keen trial; for Our Lord is the Rock in a primitive, essential, and incommunicative sense, and Peter is so called in a figurative, representative way, because he was used ministerially and instrumentally in founding the visible Church. In the same sense, though not with the same personal circumstances, the same idea is extended to all the Apostles in the Ephesians and the Apocalypse. But I did not mean to run on so far. All this seems to me to be included in the Christ Personal and Christ Mystical. I have often wished to see Richard Sibthorp again. I saw him soon after he returned from the R. C. Church, and heard much of his mind from him. Since that I have had frequent and trusty means of knowing his thoughts. If I do not make any promise, believe me that it is only

The Cardinal and the Jesuits.

from a fear of entangling myself more than I ought. But I will write to him, and ask whether we could meet. And now I will add to this nothing but my hope that every good gift may be with you, and yours, abundantly from the Father of Lights.
Believe me, always affectionately yours in Jesus Christ,
H. E. MANNING.

"WHAT AN ESCAPE MY POOR SOUL DID HAVE."

Mr. Mozley has given a wide currency to the gossip of an irresponsible moment by making "the sagacious Bishop Samuel Wilberforce" say to the Prince Consort: "If Manning had been made a Bishop he would have been with us now." When Wesley was leading a multitude after him, " Make him a Bishop" was the vulgar recipe given to heal the schism. In one case as in the other the motives and character of the men were utterly misunderstood. As, however, the story of the Archdeacon (whose ultimate preferment in the Anglican was as secure as his future in the Catholic Church was unpromising) has been repeated here and there in obituary biographies, the following little anecdote, sent to us by one who lived under the Cardinal's own roof and heard it from his own lips, is worth a record:

Shortly before Archdeacon Manning left the Establishment he was told by a member of the Government for the time being that he was to have the next vacant bishopric. Not long after his reception into the Church a see (Salisbury, I believe) fell vacant, and a Cabinet Minister meeting him said: "We should have appointed you"; to which he made the characteristic remark: "What an escape my poor soul did have!"

THE CARDINAL AND THE JESUITS.

It was by a Jesuit that Archdeacon Manning was received into the Church—Father Brownbill, in the Hill Street residence then attached to the Farm Street Church. In that church, too, he was accorded a confessional, where his friends might have ready access to him during the first year of his Catholic and priestly life. Again the Jesuits entered into his

The Cardinal and the Jesuits.

life when Father Whitty, who had been made Provost of Westminster in 1852, wished to resign his post in 1857 to enter the Society. Cardinal Wiseman at once found a new Provost in Dr. Manning. Again the Jesuits entered into his life—and quite differently. The Jesuits were to receive into their Society clergy of his own, his lothness to part with whom moved his very soul. Father John Morris, a secular priest in the year 1865, was breakfasting in a café within the shadow of Quimper Cathedral, when his eye fell on the words of a French newspaper: "*Monseigneur Manning a reçu ses bulles de Rome.*" From Brest he telegraphed: "If this news is true send me your blessing." The answer came: "Return at once: it is true, though I cannot understand it." So Father Morris returned and sat in the seat of the Archbishop's secretary. How and why he left it shall be told in his own words :*

I must now speak of a very personal matter, but for it I owe Cardinal Manning a great debt of gratitude, of which I am anxious now to pay some instalment. I was living in his house, and I was his Diocesan Secretary. An ancient desire had revived in my heart with irresistible force, and I was most anxious to be permitted to enter the Society of Jesus. In Cardinal Wiseman's time, and in the early days of Archbishop Manning, it would not have been possible. There was no one to take my place in an office that must necessarily be filled and that no one coveted. Many strings were in my hands, and unless someone else would take charge of them, I could not move. Such a one was found, and I have always looked on his coming as a special favour bestowed by God's goodness upon me. One day I said to the Archbishop that the physical labour of so much writing was too much for me. He agreed at once, and said that two priests were coming for their destinations that day, and I might have either of them to help me. He suggested one of them, and I acquiesced; but a little while afterwards I went to him, saying, "My Lord, that choice just now was a mistake. Let me have Dr. Johnson instead. I am sure that he will do." Dr. Johnson came, and it was soon clear that he could do my work far better than I

---

* From his very valuable article on "The Cardinal Archbishop" (the *Month*, February, 1892).

The Cardinal and the Jesuits.

could do it. Literally before long I was without an office, and Archbishop Manning had a Diocesan Secretary immeasurably better than I. While the Archbishop was debating with himself what he would do with me next, he went out of town, and I seized the opportunity to go to Roehampton to make a Retreat. Father Fitzsimon accepted me only on the condition that I did not trouble him, as he was busy with the long Retreat of his novices. I did not need him, for I had no sooner set foot in the chapel where the novices were making their meditation than I saw clearly—and the light, thank God, has never faded away—that the time was come and that it was God's will that I should enter the Noviceship. In consequence of Dr. Johnson's perfect fitness for my duties, Archbishop Manning *could* let me go; but *would* he? I asked Father Weld, who was then Provincial, whether he would receive me, and he said that if I came with the full consent of the Archbishop he would, but he "would not fight for me." He would take me if I were free to come; and on that supposition I asked him how long he supposed it would be before I could hope to enter the Novitiate. His answer was that if I was out of that house in six months I might consider myself fortunate. I was out of the house, with the Cardinal's full leave, in less than a month. I asked him on the Vigil of St. Andrew, 1864, and before Christmas he had let me go. That Vigil of St. Andrew I am not likely ever to forget. It was against his Grace's wish that I should leave him, and against his judgment too, for he did not believe that I had a vocation to the Religious life; but this only makes his speedy acquiescence all the more generous. I never had from him an unkind word, he never did a harsh thing in my regard; and though by my own act I separated myself from him and all his interests, he never shut me out from his friendship. I never noticed any coldness in his manner towards me at any time during these five-and-twenty years. I am fully aware that I am not saying anything complimentary to myself, if I add that the Cardinal felt it much more when his nephew, Father Anderdon, left his house and Father Humphrey left the Oblates in order to enter the Society. Those who knew his house and remember William Newman, the faithful servant who had been for many years butler to Cardinal Wiseman, and who continued in the service of Cardinal Manning—those who know what the loss of Newman was to him, will be able to appreciate the humour with which he said: "To make it quite complete, Newman should go to be a lay-brother."

The Cardinal and the Jesuits.

In the July of 1890 Father Anderdon passed away to his reward; and some "Memorials" of him were prepared for this magazine. The story of his life would have been incomplete without a reference to this episode, and the words in which it was told may be of interest now since they passed under the eyes of the Archbishop, and had his tacit approval. Speaking of Father Anderdon's departure from Ireland, the writer said:

On the Feast of St. John the Baptist, 1865, came a call to London. His uncle, having ascended the archiepiscopal throne at Westminster, at once summoned to his side the nephew to whom he had ever been as an elder brother. To York Place Father Anderdon came, taking the post of Archbishop's secretary; finding, even from that, spare hours in which to preach and to write. He was in the head-quarters of hard work—his element; and it seemed as if a link of common labour and of common love had been formed such as only death could sever. When else had so supreme a model a copy so apt? He, too, was hungry for work; and he had capacities as preacher, writer, and guide of souls, which reflected those of his chief, to whom even his face had more than a fancied resemblance. His very handwriting reproduced his master's, as another "William's" was to resemble another Cardinal's in the years to come. But a parting came at York Place under circumstances bitter to both. It was a rending of hearts, leaving a wound which time itself, in the little spaces on this side of eternity, could hardly heal. It is given to most converts to feel the pangs of an uprooting once. But Father Anderdon took them all upon himself once and again. "A wrench is good to teach detachment," he had said. That was his way of learning the necessary lesson; and he spared himself no pains in the teaching. A wrench this was in its suddenness. He sought not the counsel he had steeled himself not to accept; and he made no sign, until he suddenly said: "I am going." And he was gone.

It remains only to be added that to the then Father Rector at Roehampton, who announced the news of the death of Father Anderdon, His Eminence made the following reply:

Archbishop's House, Westminster, S.W., July, 1890.
MY DEAR FATHER SCOLES,

I thank you for your kind note giving me tidings

Oblate of St. Charles.

of a true sorrow. My dear nephew grew up from childhood as a younger brother to me, and I loved him as such. He was, as you say, and as I well know, both innocent and childlike. He must have been loved by you all for his singular goodness. His end, as you tell me, must have been in every way painless and peaceful, for he was always prepared. I need not say that my prayers in Holy Mass will be united with yours. Believe me always, my dear Father Scoles, yours affectionately,

✠ HENRY E., Card. Archbishop.

OBLATE OF ST. CHARLES.

In 1856 Dr. Manning drew up the Rule for the Oblates of St. Charles Borromeo in England, and in the following year he established the Mother-house of St. Mary of the Angels, Bayswater, where he continued to reside until he left it for 8, York Place, as Archbishop of Westminster. Father Herbert Vaughan, afterwards Bishop of Salford, and always the Cardinal's close friend, was one of the first members of the Bayswater Community; and it was his enthusiasm for St. Charles which had, we believe, in the first instance called the special attention of the ex-Archdeacon, who became the Saint's devoted lover and assiduous follower, to the great Cardinal Archbishop of Milan. Of his constant affection for that Congregation, every member of which he loved as a brother, sufficient records will be elsewhere made. We content ourselves with printing here the words in which the Very Rev. Dr. Butler, O.S.C., his beloved Father Confessor, strove to express his own feelings, and those of the Fathers, on the death of their English Founder and first Father Superior:

"*For if you have ten thousand instructors in Christ, yet not many fathers. For in Christ Jesus by the Gospel I have begotten you.*"—1 COR. iv. 15.

I have the sad privilege of speaking a few words, my dear brethren in Jesus Christ, to express rather to the ear of God than as a discourse addressed to you the depth and the keenness of

Oblate of St. Charles.

the sorrow which has fallen upon us here. A family and a home are mourning for the loss of a Father. Many have described, and in eloquent language, the nobleness of the life which God has now closed in peace and which men are recalling and storing up worthily in their memory. We may be forgiven if we come back to the early years of one so dear to us and console ourselves under an affliction deeply personal by reflecting on what we know, in some ways best of all, of the outset of such a life. We will suppress our mourning with an effort and for a few moments ask our memory to bring back the presence of our Father, rudely sketching the portrait of his mind and character. It will soon be thirty-five years since these holy walls first heard the clear and sweet tones of a voice which they will echo no more. One warm heart and one wise and eloquent tongue have endeared our home to us. Without a pause, prayer, praise of God, and the busy intercommunion of the priests and the flock have ever since been accumulating graces and holy joys, and an ever increasing sense that God loves this sanctuary of St. Mary of the Angels ; but from that evening of Our Lady's Visitation in 1857, when he first preached upon Mary, the Queen of the Angels, all this holy and happy history has been bound up with him, our Father, our Founder, and our ever vigilant Bishop. To speak so soon is a severe obedience laid upon me ; but there are two urgent reasons—(1) God is looking to see us recognise our full debt of gratitude ; and (2) our Father, whose eyes are closed to this world only, expects us to follow lovingly his precious soul with our suffrages fervent in proportion. It is far too soon for those who have lived under the powerful sway of his personal influence to turn and reflect upon that influence, so as to give an account of it and to analyse its working. And the more deeply and more strongly from long and happy intimacy we have each known its hold upon us, the more calm and more slow shall we need to be in appreciating what we have possessed. The charm will not die gradually away, because the secret of so holy a power upon our lives, of so holy a light penetrating and shining through our minds, was the breath of God's Holy Spirit, the same Divine Comforter ever present in the true pastors of God's flock, Who made the disciples of St. Paul so love him that, falling upon his neck, they kissed him, grieving most of all because of that word that they should see his face no more. One after another we have grown familiar with the alternations of his eventful life and its vast successes. We were privileged to know the purity of his motives as he set forth, the

HENRY EDWARD MANNING,
FATHER SUPERIOR OF THE OBLATES OF ST. CHARLES
AND PROTONOTARY APOSTOLIC.

(*From a Portrait at St. Charles's College, Bayswater.*)

Oblate of St. Charles.

soundness of the means upon which he laid his hand, and what it cost him to succeed. One can tell of the morning when, before he rose to go to his early Convent Mass, his hearing became affected by the anxiety of the first trials which God sent, to prove that this Community of Diocesan priests had the sign of the Cross, and therefore the blessing of the Cross, upon its foundation. Long after this he said to me, as we went together to the two Convents which we then served : "Every footstep as I take it resounds loudly through my head." He never lost the discomfort following upon that pain ; and it ended in the partial deafness of his latest years. It was in the sense of relief, at the closing of that trial, that he preached his sermons on confidence in God: one of those small cherished writings in which thousands of those suffering in mind or body, and especially the dying, have found their consolation. He preached on the love of Jesus to penitents, and his words are as a manual to many and many precious souls for whom and from whom he suffered much as he wrestled for and rescued them, one by one—God alone knows how many—during his forty years of unseen pastoral toil. "You put both your hands into the fire," I once said to him, "to rescue that poor soul." "Indeed I did," was his reply. His life could easily be divided into periods by the successive movements, generally of far reaching interest and importance, in which his gift of discovering in which direction to find a just issue or a just conclusion made him take the unpopular side. The worldly spirit inseparable from a Church established by the law of our national government brought his conscience to a crisis as soon as his power of governing men had begun to be appreciated. He declined what he used to call the first step of the ladder of preferment in that body, and prepared for the greater sacrifice of the position of authority itself which he was holding as Archdeacon Manning. We can recall in detail the two kinds of reply which he uniformly made to personal or public assaults upon him. The oft repeated text, " It hath seemed good to the Holy Ghost and to us to lay no more burthen upon you excepting these necessary things," was the beginning of that didactic exposition of the treasures of the Faith, and of the life of inward purity and outward loyalty, to which, week by week, he summoned every Christian, as London heard him in every part. Expounding the Faith was his first reply to controversial challenges. To go on more with the work of God was the second. His characteristic restless energy I leave to the eloquent to describe, both

Oblate of St. Charles.

in itself and in the copious successes with which God blessed it. But in intimate contact you perceived that in his whispers in conversation, his dreams at night, his confidences given into sympathising ears, he was the same, as the Orator, or the Ruler, or the Counsellor of Holy Church. He took to heart with a sensitiveness corresponding to his vivid insight into principles and truths the enterprises, great or small, into which he poured all that Nature and grace bestowed upon him. As he walked down a street we who knew him could detect the warmth with which he fixed his gaze on fine young English youths, capable of so much, whose souls had not the light of faith. He loved St. Paul's words : "But what then ? So that every way, whether by occasion, or by truth, Christ be preached : in this also I rejoice, yea, and will rejoice" (Phil. i. 18), although he knew full well how this arrested and perhaps shocked those who had not his fearless love of souls. No sooner was he a Bishop than he lay awake at night, thinking of the little ones that were perishing. And it was no excitement that made him often say, as he spoke of the starving peasants of Ireland: "My whole soul is with them." As God lengthened his life, He deepened his sympathy and enlarged his view of the world of souls, and his capacity of reaching and gathering them. Who does not know that his eye kindled as he detected any broader grasp of life, any brighter view of God's charity, of man's dignity, of the action of the Holy Ghost in His reign over all, or in His control of each, any more refined sympathy with the patience and sweetness of God with His little ones, little by suffering, or helplessness, or pitiable because of sin. He was a master of his own language ; but he had a rare gift added, of which he himself was only partially conscious, as his surprise will show when he found his young disciples entangled in their thoughts as well as labouring to find language. The clearness of his speech followed after the clearness of his thoughts. This appeared when in other countries he sat in conversation or debate on the great questions of Holy Church or the Supreme Pontiff. The Bishops of France, in their loyalty and their prudence, urged him to write the three Pastorals, to which, as a book, he gave the name of "Petri Privilegium." He had no sooner arrived in Rome, at the time when our beloved Pontiff Pius IX. was hastening to his crown, than before the day was out the foremost and wisest of the Cardinals of Rome came humbly to confer, to listen, and to be led. There is much which only a distant future will make known, which made the holy reigning Vicar of Christ on earth speak of him

Oblate of St. Charles.

in memorable words. The New Testament was his manual, he used to say, not for curious study, not for quotation on occasions, but for the ever fresh awakening of his mind to the full light for which he prayed—for the renewing of joyous thought and courage in the onward progress of his life and ministry. It is the principle of Holy Church in her training and guiding of the young and old of her clergy, that by ministering to God the minister becomes worthy; and therefore a self-conscious, timid, and narrow way of keeping God's law he tolerated unwillingly; but a free, self-forgetful, ever ready spirit which leaves in God's keeping the question how the *worker* fares, and presses on, not because worthy but because urged and invited by Divine charity—*that* he cherished. Prayer came of his work, as the repose and the reaction; and the worker went forth from prayer confident that He Who says "Come," can make feet of flesh walk upon the waters, even in the stormy night. He clothed himself with his work, because his work was his life; to love and to labour were one; to *lean* on God, to *presume* Him present, to give all natural gifts their full, free scope and intensity, this was his daily life. This was the sense of his maxim, "Depend on no one but God and yourself." And this brings me to a reflection which, my brethren, may be already in your minds. Was it presumption or is it presumption to follow as I have ventured to do, and as the minds and hearts of priests and faithful of St. Mary of the Angels have done, a great Archbishop and a Cardinal long removed from his humble parish? He was called to plan and accomplish for the whole Church of Westminster, of England, of the world. For the moment let me only answer, I am sure that we shall be forgiven if personal affection claimed to take as a domestic subject each and every enterprise of his life. But it is time to show that I remember that the just man is an accuser of himself in the beginning of his speech. It would have been unseemly to lift the veil and gaze upon his secret daily colloquy with God, but he frankly has used for others the very prayer with which he was every day cleansing his own soul before his God. I will venture to quote it every word. It is his soul; it is our inheritance. He once told me that for, I think, thirty years he had never missed one day to appeal thus to the Holy Spirit of God:

O God the Holy Ghost, Whom I have slighted, grieved, resisted from my childhood unto this day; reveal unto me Thy personality, Thy presence, Thy power.

Oblate of St. Charles.

Make me to know Thy seven-fold gifts,—the spirit of wisdom and understanding, of counsel and fortitude, of knowledge and piety, and of the fear of the Lord. O Thou Who art the Spirit of the Father and the Son, O Thou Who art the love of the Father and the Son, O Thou Who baptisest with fire and sheddest abroad the love of God in our hearts, shed abroad Thy love in my heart. One thing have I desired of the Lord, that will I seek after; not wealth, rank, power, worldly home, worldly happiness, or any worldly good; but one drop of that holy flame, one drop of that holy fire, to kindle me and set me all on fire with the love of my God. Let that holy flame burn up and consume in me every spot and soil of the flesh and the spirit. Purify me seven-fold with Thy gifts; receive me as a holy sacrifice wholly acceptable unto Thee; kindle me with zeal, melt me with sorrow, that I may live the life and die the death of a fervent penitent.

And now it is time for us to address ourselves, and to apply these few reflections and many more in the form of an appeal to every group and Community amongst us, and to the conscience and the charity of each one of us. I will not speak of the longing desire which he had not to be forgotten by his own, but to be followed by our multiplied and persevering prayers. I will only read the well-known words of a Saint who was specially enlightened—St. Catherine of Genoa :

I see Paradise has no gate, but that whosoever will may enter therein; for God is all mercy, and stands with open arms to admit us to His glory. But still I see that the being of God is so pure (far more than one can imagine) that should a soul see in itself even the least mote of imperfection it would rather cast itself into a thousand hells than go with that spot into the presence of the Divine Majesty. When a soul is approaching to that state of first purity and innocence which it had when created, the instinctive desire of seeking happiness in God develops itself, and goes on increasing through the fire of love, which draws it to its end with such impetuosity and vehemence that any obstacle seems intolerable, and the more clear its vision the more extreme its pain.

Let us think thus as we pray for his precious soul.

Impressions of him as a Preacher.

MADE ARCHBISHOP.

Pius IX., who had made Manning's acquaintance while he was still an Archdeacon, who had placed him in the College of Noble Ecclesiastics at Rome after his conversion, and who had made him, at Bayswater, a Doctor of Divinity and a Protonotary Apostolic, appointed him in 1865 to the Archbishopric of Westminster, vacant by the death of Cardinal Wiseman. Others had claims and supporters, notably Archbishop Errington; but precedents were set aside to place in the See one who was "a Heaven-born Archbishop." Pius IX., when he first saw Manning after his appointment, confessed that many people had opposed it: "But I had a voice in my ear that continually said to me 'Put him there, put him there!'" That no choice was made less waywardly, however, or was justified more splendidly, first and last, is the verdict of every observer, casual or close, of his rule of twenty-seven years.

MEMORIES AND PORTRAITS.

To get a precise portrait of this "Archbishop to his finger tips" baffled the wit of any painter. "If ever a man feels a fool," he used to say, "it is when the photographer uncaps his camera;" yet certain photographs give a better view of the real Manning than do such portraits as those painted by Legros and by Long. If his face was a difficult one to catch in paint, so was his personality a difficult one to portray with pen and ink. From a variety of tributes that have reached us we select such as seem to express most truly some trait of the great Archbishop, or some sentiment he inspired in others.

IMPRESSIONS OF HIM AS A PREACHER.

"One who knew him well" writes to us as follows:

I first heard him preach in Rome, at the English College, on the Feast of St. Thomas of Canterbury. He was very patriotic on that subject, very much an Englishman, very full of the liberties of the English Constitution. But no sentence suited him so well as " The Archbishop, but no traitor," when he came to the scene of the Saint's martyrdom. It was then that one's heart ratified that title as his by all the claims and all the rights. At that moment he had some dramatic fire in him. His voice was low and clear, every word was cut as finely as his own features. His syllables fell " like snow "—the phrase he himself applied to Bishop Wilberforce's and to Newman's. Seeing that Englishmen have completely lost the genius of dramatic action, it is perhaps a pity that convention should still impel them to use gesture in the pulpit. On the stage it is perhaps inevitable ; a play carried on with the uneloquent bodies, faces, voices of real life, would be a lifeless thing to see. Yet for this one little reason—that, for Englishmen, life and the drama are quite separate worlds of action—the English stage must always be the scene of distressing conventionalities, and vital acting an impossibility. But in the pulpit a man may stand and speak in his natural immovable way without the slightest offence. Cardinal Manning was English all through—English in the fibre and blood and in the habit of his temperament—and so he was incapable of natural gesture, and he therefore avoided all action in the pulpit save that of an admonitory finger. How English was his tongue, how English his throat, was shown by his " Italian " Latin. Of course, like all ecclesiastics, he had acquired what is considered to be the Italian pronunciation, and he had even taken evident pains to be very Italian indeed, as an act of homage to the Italian conditions of modern English Catholicism. His c's were Italian, and his j's, and his vowels were open. But the English tongue made of his Latin the most British thing conceivable, all the same. I never heard him speak French, but I know precisely the kind of accent he must have had. This insular trick of speech is smiled at abroad, but I love it—it is so refined and reticent.

DISTINCTION OF MANNER.

A lady, who had the honour of a long acquaintance, writes :

His courtesy to women was marked, and he always had a truly royal air of conferring distinction on the person he addressed. One thing he disliked so much that he said it affected his manners—conspicuous dress. On one occasion he averred that he had hardly had patience to finish the talk with a visitor because she was wearing a gown with very large checks in

Intended Toils.

it. He was observant in these things, and very severe on the natural vanities. He himself was placed so high above those little anxieties which are really much more common than self-complacency. He looked precisely as he must have wished to look. One wondered whether, if Nature had set his soul in a coarse and undignified person, he would have been so severely indifferent to appearances. No man accustomed to the routine of homage ever overlooked the solecisms of others with a more graceful unconsciousness. I remember introducing to him, in my own house, a lady who, though a Catholic, was not versed in the rules for greeting Princes of the Church; but no one would have guessed from the subtlest sign in his aspect that she had omitted anything. Once as I passed out of his room, I was succeeded by a non-Catholic philanthropist, and I just heard, with a little shiver, the clapping, smacking shake of the hand, and the violent, "Well, Cardinal, how *are* you?" in a cheery Nonconformist twang, to which His Eminence's reply seemed to be everything that was cordial. One heard of his coldness and hardness; there were the current stories, of course, about the Marble Arch-bishop and about having been too long with a Cardinal and taken cold: but I never saw a discouraging or repellent look in his face. Certainly, there was always a sense that in speaking, however freely, and in smiling, however gaily, he held himself somewhat removed. And in his demeanour there was always "presence"—that "air" which was so greatly esteemed in the last century: but it was a natural gift. People thought him tall, though he was of quite ordinary height; and wherever he appeared, though he had borne no titles, he would have been important.

INTENDED TOILS.

A correspondent who thinks it may comfort some to know that "even the Archbishop had unaccomplished projects," says:

Though "excitable" was the last epithet to apply to Cardinal Manning, yet he was often possessed by a new idea, or an idea newly realised, in such a manner that for a time he gave way to strong feeling, and sometimes, I may almost say, took fright. Perhaps it was about the depravity of society; or about an evil within his own fold. Catholic children attending Protestant schools—at one time he was suddenly convinced of the existence of such in their hundreds and thousands in the slums of London. He made an irresistible pulpit appeal to members of Catholic

"Gay without actual laughter."

congregations to help him to lay hands upon these children. In consequence, a number of ladies undertook to hunt in the several districts of the London parishes, and after a house-to-house visitation extremely few children were unearthed that were not more or less in touch with the local Catholic clergy. Of course, I do not know how it was with other parishes; but to judge from the results of rounds in some very bad slums, the idea was of the nature of a panic. Those who disapprove of total abstinence doubtless hold that the Cardinal's convictions as to the evils of alcohol were also touched with panic. But what panic has ever been equal to the authentic horror in this case? More than once he would talk with great feeling about some scheme, and ask me to come again to finish the subject. When I came a week later the subject had been allowed to lapse. There were no bounds to his desires and plans in well-doing, but the weariness of years and the pressure of other affairs prevented their fruition.

"GAY WITHOUT ACTUAL LAUGHTER."

The following is a tribute paid to the memory of the Cardinal by one who deeply mourns for him:

He had a habit of looking with a keen, yet composed, observation into any stranger's face; and the habit was significant of his relation to man, woman, and child who was, or who might be, of his flock. And they on their side had his face so well by heart that it seemed to them that his sermons had reached them as private exhortations, that he must know of those mental experiences of their own with which his words, spoken and written, had dealings so direct. Nor is this to be said of him merely as it might be said of any conspicuous and influential Prelate. The Gospel is hardly more certainly the singular concern of every several soul than was every several Catholic of London in singular relation with the Pastorate of the Cardinal. Perhaps no great priest has ever left a more general conviction of his spiritual austerity. Of his strictness towards himself the time has not come to speak. But this may be said now—that it never impaired his humour, or dimmed his wit, or discouraged the gay talk—gay without actual laughter—which was so frequent in times of rest. The Cardinal Archbishop had never assumed a dignity, and thus he never laid it by; and to some he seemed to keep an unrelaxed state, but it was a state in inseparable union with his nature. A stern ecclesiastic he might be, but the poor did not think so. Those who were incapable of thought or of gratitude would not have thought so—the martyr-children of London, whom he sought to save, or the animals he would have rescued from vivisection. The penitents of the streets did not think him austere, nor the inebriates, nor even any thrice unhappy who, once of the sanctuary itself, had lost their Faith and everything with it. If he was "narrow" it was that he walked in the narrow way of this difficult world; his narrowness excluded none who would walk there with him. But indeed the accusation was a foolish one, uttered by rote. In politics, in social economy, in scientific interests, the Cardinal was of exceptional liberality. Great Prelate, illustrious Englishman, devout Christian, patriot, and scholar, the second Cardinal Archbishop of Westminster leaves none but noble memories. He never spared himself in life; and death, to which he must often have sent in advance a message of welcome, spared him any hard suffering. "Il vaut bien la peine de vivre sans plaisir pour avoir le plaisir de mourir sans peine." The sentence is rather ingenious than loftily spiritual. The Cardinal did not live a hard life in the hope of avoiding pain in his last hour; he lived it for the love of God, as, we may hope, he lives the second life already.

THE APOSTOLATE OF LETTER-WRITING.

It might be thought that the Cardinal had his time and attention filled by the exercise of his private pieties and the discharge of his duties as a Diocesan. But, besides this, there was the constant succession of visitors to Archbishop's House, a door that was closed to none. Nor did the visitor ever enter that little inner room without finding on the floor a patchwork of envelopes. Not to tread on them was a matter of some agility at times. Every hour of the day letter after letter was written—an apostolate of penmanship, the extent of which will never be realised. No labour did this great disciple spare himself in the service of his Master. Not merely to friends or acquaintances, nor to strangers who applied to him direct, did these letters find their way. Perhaps a Nun who had never seen the Cardinal would write to tell him of a lady who was in some distress of body or mind, to whom a word

The Apostolate of Letter-writing.

from him would come with healing. To one such lady were the following letters, addressed. She was a recent convert then and did not feel at home in her new environment. A Nun wrote to the Archbishop stating her case, and he immediately sent her a copy of "The Temporal Mission of the Holy Ghost," and a letter asking her to call on him if she came to town. The following letters, which are placed at our disposal, will show the zeal with which he followed up even a casual case of the kind :

8, York Place, W., April 17th, 1871.
DEAR MRS. P——,

Your letter has just reached me. Be sure that I would have written, but that as yet I could not know where your perplexity begins. I feel sure that if you will read the book I sent, you will find, and be able to point out to me, where your doubts lie. Your letter shows me the general state of your mind, which appears to me to be caused by two things : the one a need of precise appreciation of the nature and grounds of faith ; and the other temptation against faith. You have faith though you think you have not. And the proof is that you are tempted against faith, which proves that you have it, and that the tempter would rob you of it, as he would of hope, charity, humility, and the like. I would ask you to do three things :

1. To read that book more than once, slowly and with prayer. It took me long to write it ; I feel sure that it needs time to read it.

2. To go on steadily and humbly. . . .

3. To mark the points in the book on which you wish me to write.

I hope that you will come to London, and that I may then be able to speak ; for writing is a slow and uncertain process. Meanwhile, I will not fail to remember you in Holy Mass. May God give you a docile and faithful heart in all things.

Believe me always,
Faithfully yours in Jesus Christ,
✠ HENRY E., Archbishop of Westminster.

8, York Place, August 23rd, 1871.
DEAR MRS. P——,

I was glad to hear from you and to know that you are better. I had hoped to see you in London; but as the time

The Apostolate of Letter-writing.

slipped away, I supposed you would not accomplish your intention this summer. It is a good sign that you cannot read the book. You have, I hope, no need of it. The book itself is the penance of a soul painfully finding the truth ; and it is good for those who, like prodigals, have left their Father's house. You are in it, and have the light of Faith, which is better than life itself. The law is not made for the just man, and that book is not written for the children of the Household of Faith. You have by grace what it proves by reason. I hope you have been persevering humbly and with gratitude in your confessions and communions. Lively faith is the love of the Sacred Heart of Jesus. May God bless and keep you in His holy fear.
    Believe me always,
      Yours faithfully in Jesus Christ,
      ✢ HENRY E., Archbishop of Westminster.

    8, York Place, W., November 13th, 1871.
MY DEAR MRS. P.———,
  I shall be most happy to see you to-morrow at any time between 10 and 12.30 ; and I hope that without any such promises you would not have gone through London without coming to me. Believe me always,
      Very truly yours,
      ✢ HENRY E., Archbishop of Westminster.

    8, York Place, W., July 28th, 1872.
MY DEAR CHILD,
  I do not think there has been any forgetfulness on your part or on mine. But I was glad to receive your letter. Its contents gave me neither surprise nor anxiety, for I understand the turns and temptations of your mind enough to account for the freaks you describe. They are of no reality. They do not come from malice, or from a will hostile to our Divine Lord, His Faith, or His Church. They are the gusts, and flaps, and flaws of the thoughts and imagination, helped by illness and a highly sensitive state. I enjoin you to think no more of them ; to do them no more ; or if you do, to confess them humbly. Our Lord knows all your care. I shall pray that God may carry you safely through the trial you speak of. I hope you will see your confessor, and have the strength and solace of Our Lord's absolution and of Holy Communion. You are not likely to be in London this year, nor I to be in the North, or I

A Talk of Ten Years ago.

should gladly offer any help I could give. Be as a child at the feet of our Divine Master. Have great confidence in Him. Contrition and confidence are enough. *No penitent soul can perish, and no soul that loves God can be lost.* Be humble and docile, and full of fidelity to the Sacred Heart of Jesus. May His blessing be with you.

Always yours very truly,

✠ HENRY E., Archbishop of Westminster.

THE READY PEN.

A priest of the Diocese of Shrewsbury writes to us :

When I was at Ushaw, in upper classes, I asked Cardinal Manning's blessing on a small religious " offering of the actions of the day." His Eminence wrote back promptly to grant my request, adding : " Practise this devotion to the Passion of Our Lord for me."

On December 10th, 1888, the same priest received the following letter :

MY DEAR FATHER,

I thank you for your kind letter, and for saying Mass for me. Thank God, I am fairly well again ; but eighty years, and my late illness, make me slow in regaining strength. Thank also the good Nuns for their prayers. The Faithful Companions are my staff officers in this diocese, and I have great confidence in them. I am truly thankful that you have found help in my little book.* May God be with you, your Flock, and the Convent. Believe me,

Yours affectionately in Jesus Christ,

HENRY E., Cardinal Archbishop.

A TALK OF TEN YEARS AGO.

The Rev. George Angus, writing to us from St. Andrews, says :

At one time when resident in Kensington, and occupying the post of Bursar at the short-lived Catholic University College, I used to see a good deal of Cardinal Manning. His Eminence

* "The Eternal Priesthood."

·A Talk of Ten Years ago.

used to sit in an armchair drawn as close as possible to the fire, his legs and feet being closer, at the risk, as I used to think, of being scorched. The Cardinal did not write at a desk or table, but on his knee, as does, I believe, Miss Braddon, the novelist. Once when I was sitting close to him he dropped his pen; I stooped to pick it up: "Never mind it," he said, "life is too short to be wasted in picking up pens"; and he took another from a bundle of quills lying on the table beside him. His Eminence used to throw down his letters, when written and in their envelopes, upon the floor; then they were gathered up and posted by the servant. Not liking such an untidy litter, I essayed one day to pick up the letters. "Don't do that," said the Cardinal, "they will never be posted if not left on the floor." I told him that I had heard that Bishop Samuel Wilberforce (his brother-in-law) used, when writing in the train, to toss his letters into an umbrella open, and placed on the floor of the carriage. "Ah!" said the Cardinal with a somewhat grim smile, "if he had never done anything worse than that——." In former days, before I became a Catholic, I was intimate with a well-known London clergyman, now dead—Edward Stuart, founder and first Vicar of St. Mary Magdalene's, Munster Square. Mr. Stuart always professed a great admiration for the Cardinal, whom he had known well as Archdeacon of Chichester, and once pointed out to me a house in Regent's Park, formerly the residence of Mr. Dodsworth, of Christ Church, Albany Street (afterwards a convert of the Catholic Church), where the Archdeacon, Mr. Dodsworth, and Mr. Stuart used to meet and take counsel regarding Anglican affairs. At one time Mr. Stuart had been on the point of becoming a Catholic, but having met Archdeacon Manning somewhere on a journey (if I remember rightly), was dissuaded from leaving the "Church of his baptism" by the Archdeacon. I told Cardinal Manning of this, and asked if it was true? "Quite true," was the reply, "and may God forgive me for it." Cardinal Manning had a great aversion to the use of tobacco, whether in the shape of smoking or of snuff. Once in my presence, when the Cardinal was speaking ·to a priest, the Reverend Father, in an unguarded moment, produced a silver snuff-box and regaled himself with a pinch. "Give me that box," said His Eminence. The priest meekly handed it over to the Cardinal, who put it in his pocket. Whether the priest ever regained his snuff-box, I do not know. His Eminence perferred plain song in church, and much disliked the other music commonly used. He was wont to say

As Dissenters saw him.

" I can always make a better act of faith when I hear the *Credo* sung to Gregorian music." I once ventured to point out that, in this matter, the churches in Rome often set a very bad example. " Too true," rejoined the Cardinal, " and what is the consequence ? Victor Emmanual is at the Quirinal." I happened to be with the Cardinal in the sacristy of a London church when some very elaborate and florid music was being performed which I knew the Cardinal disliked. A priest present asked His Eminence what he thought of some decorations in the church ? " I'll tell you what I think of your music," said the Cardinal; " it is diabolical." " An English gentleman," His Eminence once remarked to me, " should know his Aristotle, and ride to hounds." Cardinal Manning's carriage was—as I recollect it— of a very unassuming, I might say shabby, appearance. I expressed my wish that His Eminence had a nicer turn-out, as befitted a Prince of the Church. " That is all very well," he rejoined ; " but sometimes when people drive in fine coaches they drive to the devil."

AS DISSENTERS SAW HIM.

The Rev. Benjamin Waugh, the Nonconformist minister who has devoted himself to the rescue of suffering childhood, was sure by all titles to win a welcome from the Cardinal. To Mr. Waugh, though he had a "strong constitutional and principled dislike" of the Catholic Church, the Cardinal's "sweetness and sanctity " seemed those of a child.

He was a king. His robes and jewels, and shields and heraldry, and tower of strength were that his great mind and heart went out to his race. He was at the summit of all the humanity you had known. Your reverence for him sprang from the glimmer of himself in you. There was a deep, tender fear in it which was akin to worship, and which tended to make men of no religion and men of every variety of religion, kneel for his blessing as Jacob's sons knelt for Jacob's. To this personality was added the subtle suggestion of his coming to you from a still larger world than the vast world of men. In all his bearing was the saying : "I am a stranger and sojourner with you." He was a son of the living God and Father of all. Men, rude and refined, of his Church, of no Church, and of all Churches, while revering and loving him for himself, had their unbelief put

HENRY EDWARD MANNING,
ARCHBISHOP OF WESTMINSTER AND CARDINAL OF THE
HOLY ROMAN CHURCH.
(From a Photograph by Elliott & Fry.)

"A little child shall lead them."

a little to shame, or their faith gladdened, by the subtle, luminous power in which his strong, clear faith and joy in his God and theirs bathed him, and, for the moment, them. They had seen none such wonderful manhood. The sense of eternal things which filled his presence, men, to their surprise, felt in a degree haunting themselves. They had glimmers of a nimbus around his venerable head which made them, perhaps, dimly understand why painters had gilded aureoles around the heads of those Saints which hung upon his walls. Yet not the humblest docker, not the youngest child, not the hardest unbeliever, found in him any "greatness," as earth's great personages are great. He had the gentleness, the deference of a father pitying his children. He was aware not in the least that he was a Cardinal Archbishop : to be of service to you seemed the special object of his life. It was thus that "My son," as he used to address an earnest man, seemed so well to become his lips. Yet was his pleasure in his service so child-like, that his heart seemed to bound and sing with the enjoyment of the thought that he could be anything of a helper to the helpless among men.

"A LITTLE CHILD SHALL LEAD THEM."

The same writer, in his "Reminiscences of Cardinal Manning," in the *Contemporary Review* (February, 1892) tells these stories :

His interest in children was like his character—an all-round one, and of the most genuine and simple kind. "I like to go into the parks on Sunday," he said on one occasion, "to see the children and talk with them ; and I give them my blessing." Then, with a pleased smile, he added : "Nobody can say that I am proselytising in that." Referring on one occasion to a depressed remark I had made to him on the small results of the past year's work: "Only seventy cases!" he exultingly exclaimed. "Small result! Think of seventy little children's tears dried, and seventy little children's pains stopped! We can never say that that is nothing. It is glorious!" In a still more solemn voice, he continued : "A child's needless tear is a blood-blot upon this earth." A worker for the Society, after a tour in Ireland, called upon him, at his request, to tell him the result. On hearing that the Catholic priest and the treasurer of the Irish Church Missionary Society, Parnellite and Mc-Carthyite, Orangeman and Home Ruler, had met together on

The Scarlet Gentleman.

our platform, and had joined in forming our Aid Committees, he clapped his hands and exclaimed: "How happy the old prophet would have been! The good days are coming. It is the little child that will be their leader. People will find their brotherhood in little children." On one occasion he told me this story in slow periods, in which every word was a reality: "I was going down that street," pointing out of the window to a double row of mansions that were being built, "and I met a little boy going along his happy way, with poor dress, but a lovely, thoughtful, pale, open face; and I stopped him for the pleasure of speaking to him. 'Well, my little man, how are you, and where are you going with that little bundle in your hand?' He told me 'there'—pointing to one of the houses being built, 'to his father.' 'What is your father?' I asked. 'A carpenter, Sir,' he replied." Then the Cardinal added slowly, "I was awed and startled! I had met a carpenter's son! My Lord was once a little servant like that boy. Oh, Mr. Waugh," he exclaimed, almost in tears, "what depths of love were in Christ!" He then in the simplest way disclosed that he had at once returned home and sent all that he had then to give to some institution for the children of the poor. "I feel at times," he said, "ashamed to own anything." I saw in that moment how intense upon him was the power of the life of Our Lord.

THE SCARLET GENTLEMAN.

Mrs. Sheldon-Amos, a philanthropic lady of strong Protestantism, went to the Cardinal for advice on one occasion; and having heard much of him from others, she was "not surprised to find how sweetly genially humorous he was—in fact, half-chaffing on some subjects, while burning with indignation on others." Other interviews followed, all most pleasant to her to remember, although she was perhaps a little apt to fancy that her Protestantism was under attack. It is so easy if you are talking to a Cardinal to see at each turn the eager proselytiser. The Cardinal always noted with a smile this nervousness on the part of sensitively Protestant visitors, but it did not displease him. Mrs. Sheldon-Amos tells, in the *Contemporary Review* (February, 1892), the story of one such interview:

At the end of my business he said: "Have you seen So-

The Scarlet Gentleman.

and-so (a recent 'vert to the Catholic Church) lately?" I said I had, and that I was charmed to see what his Christianity could do for an Agnostic. "Yes, that is a true conversion. That is a true conversion—a conversion as you Methodists understand it, too." And presently he seemed to think this was his first good chance with me, and said, "And when are you coming nearer?" "I am not likely ever to come nearer in the sense I think you mean," I said; and he urged on me the benefits of confession. I must say that I did little but parry the attack, because I could not bring myself to say plainly what I thought. He seemed too good and gentle to be opposed. But he gave me a book of his, and asked me to discuss it with him later on. The next time he saw I was unwilling, and said nothing till we had said good-bye. Then came a pause, and "Well?" I said, "No. I only came to you for the business we have settled." "Very well, very well. But you know you need guidance." I avoided the whole question, and for a time or two he left all such personalities alone. Then he gave me a little book on the Office of the Holy Spirit, and pressed me for comments on it. At last I frankly told him that his dignity and kindness about other things made it painful to speak plainly, but that I agreed with his book as far as he could quote Scripture in support of his teaching, but that he presently came to his doctrine of the Church, and had no quotations, and that then I differed. He said gently, "You do not see your need of confession and of the Church, but it is there." I said, "No. You suggest to me means by which to get what I have already—peace with God through Jesus Christ, and access to God by the Holy Spirit. You have really nothing better to offer me. And I can say this freely to you, because you understand life as no ordinary priest can. You have lived a complete life, and understand. You know that I have all I need." He said quickly, with a sharp look at me, "Are you content with yourself then?" Of course I said no, but with the faith and doctrine I had received. And I added again: "You *know* I have what satisfies my soul's needs." He paused, nodded his head repeatedly, and then said: "I know that I think that you would always follow the truth." I said, "More than that. You know that I see the truth differently from you, and that I have what satisfies me, while you have what satisfies you. Forgive me; I must speak plainly when you press me." He turned to me, and said very solemnly: "The Church has a doctrine of the intention of the heart."

Room for General Booth.

"BUT YOU LADIES ARE TORPEDOES."

The same lady took the Cardinal to task on another occasion in a letter, and she got a letter in revenge:

I thought that in his remarks on the Encyclical he had fallen into the almost universal clerical error of laying the burden of parental responsibility on mothers. I wrote to him, saying plainly that I thought that the [Anglican] clergy generally said this sort of thing naturally; because if they returned to the earlier doctrine that it is incumbent on fathers to teach their children as they walk in the way, they would have to practise what they preached, and society pressed in the opposite direction. I begged him, from his freer position, to set the example of a better doctrine, and to try to stir fathers up to do their share. I told him I despaired of true doctrine until women took their place in pulpits and on platforms. He quickly replied:

"I began reading your letter without knowing from whom it came, and I said to myself, 'Hey-day, here is a fine lady scolding! I wonder who it is.' I then looked at the end, and wondered no longer. What can be more unjust than you? I was writing not against the women, but against employers. Mothers are partly driven into work, as you say, by the selfishness of fathers and the temptation of employers. What have I been doing for twenty years but preaching to fathers, in pledging them to total abstinence from drink, and in binding them to spend all they earn on their homes, by which the mothers can live a domestic life? Even the context of what you quote contains all this. But you ladies are torpedoes, and not legislators or preachers. There! I have had my revenge. But how can our people have homes until the land laws and the house property laws have been revised? I hope you are getting a good holiday."

ROOM FOR GENERAL BOOTH.

As "a work of human benevolence" the social undertaking of the Salvation Army had the Cardinal's warm sympathy. His Eminence, who wrote to thank "dear General Booth" for his book, and who received him at Archbishop's House, drew up in 1890 a statement of his views, in which he says:

Who that cares for human misery and human ruin can forbid

AN EMPTY CHAIR AT ARCHBISHOP'S HOUSE,
JANUARY 14, 1891.

Room for General Booth

others to do what they cannot do themselves? General Booth has at his command a vast organisation of devoted men and women ready to go and wade in the midst of this dead sea of human suffering. And it is only by human sympathy and human voices appealing, face to face, with these outcast and ruined souls, that they can be won back again to human life and to the law of God. If General Booth can gather under human influence and guidance those whom all our other agencies for good have not yet reached, who shall forbid him? If his zeal shall rebuke the indolence of some, and shall restore those whom others have rejected, and recall to order and rectitude those who have been passed by as hopeless and worthless, it is a salutary lesson to be thankfully learned. If sheep are lost it is the shepherd's fault. He may have been sleeping or dreaming in a fool's paradise, or sounding his pastoral music in a refined life of blameless morality without a shadow of the Cross: or to come nearest to the reality, he may have inherited a work which the neglect of his forefathers has put beyond his reach. How could East London have ever existed if authorities—religious, civil, municipal, parochial, social, domestic, and personal—had not been asleep, or, if awake, culpably neglectful of duty? If General Booth can reclaim this no-man's-land, where the name of God is unknown, we will wish him in reward the fulness of all grace and truth. Lastly, General Booth's work is both like and unlike all that has hitherto been attempted. It is irrelevant to point out how much has been already done, and is doing by others. They have not done all, and they cannot do all: and they have not the means to cover the whole instant and urgent need. In providing for those whom others cannot reach, he will not clash with any existing work. Moreover, he has a trained body of agents ready for the work. The man-power and the woman-power of others is neither sufficient in numbers, nor trained to a life of exceptional hardness. Let him try his hand, and if he fail, let others do better. Above all, it is intolerable to hinder General Booth in feeding the starving, and reclaiming the criminal of this day, because in the next generation a normal state of capital and labour may provide employment for posterity. In the meanwhile, must they starve? Again, it is a feeble criticism to say that in all his proposed work there is nothing new. Old needs can be met by old remedies; bread will still stay hunger, clothing keep out the cold, and work earn wages. If the scale of the application be adequate, the work is done. And for the means to make these remedies adequate he is now appealing.

For the Worthless.

It may be of interest to record that Lord Ripon, in sending a handsome subscription to the Home Colony of General Booth, did so only after consultation with Cardinal Manning.

FOR THE WORTHLESS.

To a visitor who in 1890 talked with the Cardinal upon the provision of work for the unemployed by public authorities, His Eminence said :

I am strongly of opinion that it is the duty of every commonwealth, in times of exceptional distress, such as the cotton famine in Lancashire some years ago, or exceptionally hard winters by which tens of thousands of able-bodied and deserving workmen are thrown out of work, and are reduced with their families to want and great suffering—in such cases it is the duty of public authorities, to which such affairs may appertain, to provide relief; and, in my opinion, the best relief in such cases would be in the form of employment upon works of public utility. This was the opinion of political economists such as the late John Stuart Mill and the late Professor Fawcett, although I am sorry to say certain writers at this time, with shallow philosophy, have in newspaper letters considered it a mischievous error. I will go further and say that this principle of giving food or work is embodied in the old statute law, and prevails in the spirit of our laws to this day. The 5 Elizabeth, cap. 3, appointed overseers of the poor, and made it penal to give money to any rogue or vagabond or sturdy beggar ; but it provided relief for those who are "whole and mighty in body and able to labour." The 18 Elizabeth, cap. 3, runs as follows : " To the intent that youth may be accustomed and brought up in labour and work and not grow to be idle rogues, and to the intent also that such as be already grown up in idleness, and so are rogues at present, may not have any just excuse in saying that they cannot get service or work and be then without means of livelihood, and that poor and needy persons may be set to work "—the Act goes on to provide that in " every city, town, and market, and market town, authorities should be enjoined to order a competent stock of wool, hemp, flax, or other stuff by taxation of all ; so that every poor and needy person, old or young, able to work and standing in need of relief, shall not fear want of work, go abroad begging, or committing pilfering, or living in idleness." Let it be noted that these provisions are made for the worthless; how much more does the spirit of these enactments intend that relief should be given in times of exceptional distress to the honest, able workman, skilled or unskilled, who through no fault of his own is reduced to distress! I know all that has been said about not disturbing the labour market, and not retarding the happy day when employment and labour shall be so balanced that there shall be no unemployed; but I contend that to suffer the worthy and deserving to remain wretched and starving in times of distress, which they have in no way brought upon themselves, and for which they cannot be considered responsible, but which arise from the vicissitudes of nature or of their own honest industries—to suffer them to starve would be a crime in a Christian commonwealth. It is terrible work, terrible work (said His Eminence in conclusion), and we are tyrannised over by a certain school of political economists, which makes the remedy all the more difficult to obtain.

THE PEACE SOCIETY.

A Peace Society deputation had an interview with the Cardinal Archbishop, at the end of 1890. One of those present —Mr. Thomas Snape, President of the Liverpool Peace Society —writes:

We arrived in front of a large, square mansion, and were admitted by a man-servant,' in plain livery, to the hall. Thence we were conducted up a flight of stone, uncarpeted steps, and by a corridor into a lofty reception-room, the plainness of whose furniture was in keeping with the other appearances of the house that we had seen. Library shelves, filled with ancient volumes of patristic literature, in faded bindings, covered one side of the room. An unframed canvas—a well-executed portrait, in oils, of the late Cardinal Newman—reposed against the bookcase. A well-worn carpet covered about three parts of the room. A pedestal, surmounted by a sculptured bust of Cardinal Manning himself, stood on the boards beyond. A good coal fire, in an old fashioned grate, blazed out a cheerful and grateful welcome, for the day was cold and wet. The attendant had taken our cards and letter of introduction, and presently, through another door than that by which we had come, the Cardinal entered the room. Bidding us be seated, and seating himself in an armchair near, retaining his biretta in hand, he soon engaged us in an interesting conversation upon the object of our visit. He had, he said, the fullest sympathy with the desire to promote peace and substitute arbitration for war. He was himself a Vice-President of a Peace Society. In the general conversation which followed, we pointed out to the Cardinal that the Peace Society we represented was originally founded by members of the Society of Friends; and, though not now confined to them, was still largely indebted to them for support. Cardinal Manning then spoke to us in the warmest terms of his appreciation of the Society of Friends. It was a Quaker, he said, who had given Father Mathew the Temperance pledge; it was the Quakers who had originated the Anti-Slavery Society and the Aborigines' Protection Society. He took blame to himself that in these and similar efforts so little help had been given them from outside. Though we were in the presence of a Prince of the Roman Catholic Church, and a man of high intellectual distinction apart from his high dignity, we were most courteously and affably received, and we came away greatly encouraged by the evident sympathy of Cardinal Manning with our work.

AN IRISH WOMAN'S IMPRESSIONS.

Miss Katharine Tynan, whose poetry the Cardinal greatly admired, writes of a visit paid to Archbishop's House in the September of 1889:

Presently the Cardinal came in, a tall old man and thin to attenuation, with the face of a Saint, colourless and ascetic, in which the eyes, full of kindness, smiled for the stern mouth. He was attired in a long cassock trimmed with the red of his Cardinalate, and on his thin silver hair there was a scarlet skull-cap. As he seated himself in an armchair he drew his Irish visitor a chair by his left hand with a gesture of fatherly kindness. One felt filled with a mixture of awe and reverent affection for him. He was tired with the labour and anxiety of the strike, and leaned back in his chair, looking very frail. His strength must be far greater than its seeming, or he could never get through the work he does. He talked first of poetry, mentioning among recent poetry which had interested him, that of Mr. Arthur Symons, whose "Days and Nights," dealing, as they often do, with painful social problems, would naturally interest so great a social reformer as the Cardinal. Other poetry

which he mentioned with much appreciation was that of
Mrs. Hamilton King. Presently he branched off to other topics.
Ireland, lying near his heart, easily came uppermost. He spoke
of the goodness of her people. Before the Royal Commission
on the Housing of the Poor it had been proved, he instanced,
that in the most extreme cases of poverty and overcrowding no
such evils had arisen as in other countries; drink was the only
trouble, and the drink question seemed to lie heavily on him.
He referred with satisfaction to the Temperance work being done
in Cork by Mrs. Barry and her helpers. He said the Irish made
homes under the protection of God, and no enemy came to break
through except drunkenness. "Men," said the Cardinal, "can
build houses, but only God can build a home." Then he
branched away to the newspaper press, and what it was doing,
with especial reference to the Catholic press. The doings of a
certain class of anti-Irish English Catholics and its mouthpieces
in the Press must needs vex his heart. The *Weekly Register*, he
said with emphasis, "never offends." My friend had brought
him a newspaper cutting which purposed to give an authentic
account of his way of living—how he had a farm in the country
whence came fowls and eggs and butter for his table—a pretty
fiction over which His Eminence smiled as he read it. "There
is my only farm," he said, pointing to the desolate plot of build-
ing ground outside. The news of yet another Whitechapel
horror seemed to move him deeply; his face took on a new
pallor, if that be possible, and as he closed his eyes, in pain
and horror, he looked like a Saint whose reward is already
come. The sin and misery of the great city must lie
heavily at his heart, though scarcely any other man has done
as much to lessen the burden. I thought of what Lord
Shaftesbury's son wrote when his father lay dead: "I often
heard my father say of you that wherever there was good to be
done and evil to be fought he was always sure of you." One
carried away two impressions from the Cardinal—his stateliness
and his meekness. He never for a moment was less than a
Prince, and there was an atmosphere of Royalty about him which
might well be missing in the Courts of this world, so that the
recipient of his sweetness felt at the heart a little throb of
passionate loyalty with the reverence and love which went out
to answer his graciousness. He did more to reconcile the English
Protestant mind to the idea of priesthood than all the generations
of priests who went before him. To the most unlikely places—
social gatherings, and public meetings, and into the hives of men

A Hope Unfulfilled.

—he went carrying his Master's standard, and drawing eyes and hearts to follow it. He had the fullest possible life—the life of the world and the life of the cloister alike were open books to him. He had travelled through many prosperities and many trials to this grey palace of his, whither went the prayers and heart-beats of his spiritual children in London, and the myriad of his spiritual children elsewhere, who were so through love and loyalty.

A HOPE UNFULFILLED.

An American visitor to the Cardinal at the end of 1887 made the following record of the talk:

In speaking of English politics, he said it was probable that no people were better satisfied with the structure of their Government and its institutions than those of Great Britain. In no Government in the world was there such a degree of absolute personal liberty as in Great Britain. One never knew there was any law until he ran against it. Scotland and England were completely fused in identity of interest. It was different with Ireland, because of the different treatment. That unhappy island had been ruled by England for more than three centuries by force alone. It was under Henry VIII. that the policy was inaugurated which had made and kept Ireland disaffected. Had it not been for this, Ireland would have been as devoted and as loyal to the English crown as Scotland. He was an Englishman to the backbone, but he knew and loved the Irish people. A more true, a more loyal, and a more noble race never existed. In his view the legislative body to be created for Ireland should not be one with the prerogatives of a Parliament as commonly understood, but a chamber which should have the control of legislation affecting local matters only. I said to him I had found no sentiment worth speaking of in London in favour of Irish Home Rule, and inquired what he thought about its prospects. He replied that London was intensely aristocratic, intensely wedded to custom, and therefore opposed to change. But it was not so in the Provinces. The feeling in favour of Home Rule was growing rapidly every day in the country, and he had the strongest belief it would eventually be strong enough to control both Houses of Parliament and force justice to be done to the Irish. He could not venture to predict when this day would come, but he hoped to see it.

THE VACANT CHAMBER AT ARCHBISHOP'S HOUSE,
FEBRUARY, 1892.

Verse from East and West.

VERSE FROM EAST AND WEST.

The death of Cardinal Manning, on the 14th January, 1892, and within a few hours of that of the Duke of Clarence, gave to poets and to pressmen a ready contrast between the old Prince of the Church and the young Prince of the State. This note sounds alike in the doggerel sung among his "dear dockers"— sufficiently characteristic to be here reproduced—and in the lines forwarded to us by Sir John Croker Barrow, between whom and the Cardinal was a long intimacy. In the pages of MERRY ENGLAND Mr. Francis Thompson wrote an article on "Catholics in Darkest England" which caused the Cardinal to send for him to receive his personal thanks and congratulations; an interview alluded to at the beginning of the poem now printed "To the Dead of Westminster."

SONNET.

BY SIR JOHN CROKER BARROW, BART.

On Church and State hangs one same purple pall,
    Love-wove by hands of Lord and Commoner,
    All way from Sandringham to Westminster,
For youthful Prince, and ageful Cardinal!
Rest they in peace of Death! each wept by all—
    By royal Prince and loyal Minister—
    By Guild of Capital and Labourer—
By League Conservative and Liberal.
Pray we for them! May we not further pray,
    That he, from age transainted into youth,
Will still, in spirit, guide us on our way
    Towards the threshold of Eternal Truth?
Though farther gone, yet seems he nearer grown,
For "face to face," he knows "as he is known."

Reprint of an East End Leaflet.

(*Reprint of an East End Leaflet.*)

Lines on
THE DEATH
OF
Cardinal Manning.

Tune—Lived together.

We grieve for the loss of bold Archbishop Manning,
There's many will miss every hair of his head,
And the bold Duke of Clarence beloved by the nation,
In country and town they say prayers for the dead.
We honour their names with true love and devotion,
In memory they'll live for some time to come,
And the soldiers and sailors that's ploughing the ocean,
With hearts like a lion, shed tears every one.

Chorus—

But they've gone for ever, gems together,
And bitter tears are shed,
With fond effection and recollection,
For those that's laying dead,
With sympathy we say God rest their souls today
The brave young duke and Cardinal,
Its filling us all with dismay.

What can we say, can we ever describe,
It seems as though magic had woven a spell,
In so short a time to be called by their maker,
The young Duke of Clarence and Cardinal Manning.
Eyes red with crying, and hearts fairly broken,
Will gather ere long round the tomb of the dead,
To take a last look and drop many a token,
On their mortal remains as the prayers will be said.

He worked with a will, for the good of the people
Helping the Dockers when they were in need,
He knew their distress and the way they were treated,
A good hearty soul, the Cardinal indeed,
So dearly beloved, and a friend to the people.
We honor his name and regret the sad change,
The bells will be tolling in many a steeple,
With love and respect to his mortal remains.

Such a generous soul, when in life ever ready,
To render assistance to those in distress,
In the temperance cause he was upright & steady.
The love that we bear, no tongue can express,
To rest thee in peace there's a mightier power,
Who judges us all in our time so they say,
I'm sure that he's gone to the beautiful bower,
There happiness reigns and the clouds pass away.

J. HAYDON.

The Dead of Westminster.

TO THE DEAD OF WESTMINSTER.
BY FRANCIS THOMPSON.

I will not perturbate
Thy Paradisal state
    With praise
    Of thy dead days;

To the new-heavened say,—
"Spirit, thou wert fine clay:"
    This do,
    Thy praise who knew.

I saw thee only once;
Although thy gentle tones,
    Said soft,—
    "Come hither oft."

Therefore my spirit clings
Heaven's porter by the wings,
    And holds
    Its gated golds

Apart, with thee to press
A private business;—
    Whence,
    Deign me audience.

Your singer did not come
Back to that stern bare home:
    He knew
    Himself and you.

The Dead of Westminster.

I saw, as seërs do,
That you were even you ;
    And—why,
  I too was I.

Both in the world, not of it,
I scorned, but you could move it :
    My wall,
  Material,

And inward, like yours bare.
Too far alike we were,
    Too far
  Dissimilar.

I, in weak wayfaring,
Do need the poets' spring,
    Do prize
  Some human eyes.

You smelt the Heaven-blossoms,
And all the sweets embosoms
    The dear
  Uranian year.

You saw the tender eyes
Which light the upper skies,
    With blood
  Filled on the Rood.

The carpet was let down
(With golden moultings strown)
    For you
  Of the angels' blue.

The Dead of Westminster.

But I, ex-Paradised,
The shoulder of your Christ
    Find high
    To lean thereby.

I on a lower plane
Walk in acquainted pain ;
    And take
    It for mistake,

If any sweet surprise
Of undreamed respite rise,
    And say—
    " Be glad to-day ! "

Life is a coquetry
Of Death, which wearies me,
    Too sure
    Of the amour ;

A tiring-room where I
Death's divers garments try,
    Till fit
    Some fashion sit.

It seemeth me too much
I do rehearse for such
    A mean
    And single scene.

The sandy glass hence bear—
Antique remembrancer ;
    My veins
    Do spare its pains.

The Dead of Westminster.

With secret sympathy
My thoughts repeat in me
  Infirm
  The turn o' the worm.

Beneath my appointed sod ;
The grave is in my blood ;
  I shake
  To winds that take

Its grasses by the top ;
The rains thereon that drop
  Perturb
  With drip acerb

My subtly answering soul ;
The feet across its knoll
  Do jar
  Me from afar.

As sap foretastes the spring ;
As Earth ere blossoming
  Thrills
  With far daffodils,

And feels her breast turn sweet
With the unconceivèd wheat ;
  So doth
  My flesh forcloathe

The abhorrèd spring of Dis,
With seething presciences
  Affirm
  The preparate worm.

The Dead of Westminster.

I have no thought that I,
When at the last I die,
   Shall reach
   To gain your speech.

But you, should that be so,
May very well, I know,
   May well
   To me in hell

With recognising eyes
Look from your Paradise—
   " God bless
   Thy hopelessness ! "

Call, holy soul, O call
The hosts angelical,
   And say,—
   " See, far away

" Lies one I saw on earth ;
One stricken from his birth
   With curse
   Of destinate verse.

" What place doth He ye serve
For such sad spirit reserve,—
   Given,
   In dark lieu of Heaven,

" The impitiable Dæmon,
Beauty, to adore and dream on,
   To be
   Perpetually

The Dead of Westminster.

"Hers, but she never his?
He reapeth miseries,
    Foreknows
      His wages woes;

"He lives detachèd days;
He serveth not for praise;
    For gold
      He is not sold;

"Deaf is he to world's tongue;
He scorneth for his song
    The loud
      Shouts of the crowd;

"He asketh not world's eyes;
Not to world's ears he cries;
    Saith,— 'These
      Shut, if ye please;'

"He measureth world's pleasure,
World's ease, as Saints might measure;
    For hire
      Just Love entire

"He asks, not grudging pain;
And knows his asking vain,
    And cries—
      'Love! Love!' and dies;

"In guerdon of long duty,
Unowned by Love or Beauty;
    And goes—
      Tell, tell, who knows!

"Aliens from Heaven's worth,
Fine beasts who nsoe i' the earth,

The Dead of Westminster.

  Do there
  Reward prepare.

" But are *his* great desires
Food but for nether fires?
  Ah me,
  A mystery!

" Can it be his alone,
To find, when all is known,
  That what
  He solely sought

" Is lost, and thereto lost
All that its seeking cost?
  That he
  Must finally,

" Through sacrificial tears,
And anchoretic years,
  Tryst
  With the sensualist?

" He wrought the gift, pursued
The love, by God imbued;
  May this
  Lead to the abyss?"

So ask; and if they tell
The secret terrible,
  Good friend,
  I pray thee send

Some high gold embassage
To teach my unripe age.
  Tell!
  Lest my feet walk hell.

BIBLIOGRAPHY OF CARDINAL MANNING.

At the instance of the Compiler of these Memorials, Cardinal Manning, only a few weeks before his death, prepared the following list of his published works, assisted in the task by one of his closest friends. The early volumes are now nearly all out of print; and some of them are marked at fancy prices in the second-hand catalogues. The writings of his Catholic life are published mostly by Messrs. Burns and Oates, a firm with which he began to have relations when he was Archdeacon of Chichester, and when Mr. James Burns was a prominent Anglican. While he refused to reprint the books of Anglican days—though finding little or nothing in them to repudiate—he had a hope that those of his Catholic life would always remain within reach of readers. These copyrights passed, by his will, to his executors, to whom also was assigned the charge of all his papers and correspondence. The executors are three of his beloved Oblates of St. Charles (Dr. Butler, Dr. Richards, Father Dillon) and the head of the House of Expiation in Chelsea—Canon Keens. With these old and trusted friends will lie the responsibility of deciding in what form the mass of interesting correspondence at their disposal shall be given to the world.

PUBLICATIONS DURING HIS ANGLICAN LIFE.—1835-45.

Date.	Title of Work.	Form.	Editions.
1835	The English Church—its Succession and Witness for Christ	Sermon	
,,	Address to the Archbishop of Canterbury on Synods, etc.		
,,	Sketch of the origin of Canonical Synods, etc.		
1838	Principle of the Ecclesiastical Commissioners Examined	Letter	
June 13, 1838	The Rule of Faith	Sermon (preached Chichester Cathedral)	

Bibliography of Cardinal Manning.

PUBLICATIONS DURING HIS ANGLICAN LIFE.—1835-45. (*Continued.*)

Date.	Title of Work.	Form.	Editions.
1838	The Rule of Faith (Appendix) ...		
May 31, 1838	National Education	Sermon	
1840	Preservation of Unendowed Canonries	Letter (to Bishop of Chichester)	
„	Essay on the Cathedral Act		
1841	Sanctity of Consecrated Places	Sermon Whitsuntide	
„	Moral Design of the Apostolic Ministry	Sermon (Ordination at Chichester)	
'41, '42, '45, '46, '48, '49	Charge to Clergy of Archdeaconry of Chichester		
„	The Mind of Christ the perfection and Bond of the Church	Sermon	
Nov. 27, 1842	Blessings and Duties of those who have put on Christ	Sermon (preached St. Botolph, Bishopsgate)	
1843	Visitation Charge...		
Sept. 26, 1843	Christ, our Rest and King	Sermon (preached York)	
Sept. 28, 1843	Report of Meeting, S.P.G.		
1844	Additional Bishoprics	Essay Eng. Review	
1841 to 1849	Charges Delivered at Chichester		
1841	Fund for Endowing Colonial Bishoprics, (p. 20)		
„	The Bliss of Heaven		
1842	Frequent Communion		
1842	Reasons for Daily Services		
1842 to 1844	Sermons before the University of Oxford :—		
1842	(1) The Danger of Sinning in the midst of Privileges	Sermon	
Nov. 20, 1842	(2) The Probation of the Church	„	
Mar. 12, 1843	(3) The Work appointed us	„	
Nov. 5, 1843	(4) Christ's Kingdom not of this World	„	
1843	(5) Love : the Preparation for Christ's Coming	Sermon Advent	
1844	(6) The Beatific Vision	SS. Philip James's Sermon	

Bibliography of Cardinal Manning.

PUBLICATIONS DURING HIS ANGLICAN LIFE.—1835—45. (*Continued.*)

Date.	Title of Work.	Form.	Editions.
1844	(7) The Gift of Illumination	Sermon (preached Trinity Sunday)	
1843	Festivals and Fasts		
May 8, 1844	Penitents and Saints (Sermon on behalf of Magdalen Hospital)...	Sermon	
1844	Review of Dr. Grant's Bampton Lectures on Missions...		
1846	Christ's Presence the Support of Faith		
,,	Work of the Comforter...		
,,	The Literary Fund (p. 27)		
,,	Society for the Propagation of the Gospel (p. 41)		
,,	Church in the Colonies (p. 19)		
1847	Work of Mercy for Lent...		
1848	The Lost Sheep (Opening of St. Paul's, Brighton)	Sermon	
,,	Self-sacrifice	,,	
1850	Appelate Jurisdiction of the Crown in matters Spiritual	Letter	
	Sermons in 4 Volumes.		
1848	Vol. I.　⎫　*Written in 1840.*		7 Editions
	Vol. II.　⎟　*Editions every*		4 Editions
	Vol. III.　⎬　*year up to 1850.*		3 Editions
1850	Vol. IV.　⎭　*Ten in all*		2 Editions
1845	Unity of the Church (Continuation of Mr. Gladstone's book)		2 Editions

Bibliography of Cardinal Manning.

PUBLICATIONS DURING HIS CATHOLIC LIFE.—1852-88.

Date.	Title of Work.	Form.	Editions.
1852	Grounds of Faith	Four Lectures in St. George's Southwark	9 Editions
	Confidence in God		
1866	Temporal Power of the Pope		3 Editions
1871	Fourfold Sovereignty of God		3 Editions
	Four Great Evils of the Day		
1867	England and Christendom	Letter to Dr. Pusey (Reprint)	
1865	Temporal Mission of the Holy Ghost		4 Editions
1863-73	Sermons on Ecclesiastical Subjects	3 Vols.	
1889	Lost Sheep Found	Sermon	
	Sin and its Consequences		7 Editions
1864	The Blessed Sacrament: the Centre of Immutable Truth	”	
1877	Independence of the Holy See		2 Editions
1875	Internal Mission of the Holy Ghost		5 Editions
1877-88	Miscellanies	3 Vols.	
1871	Petri Privilegium		
1877	True Story of the Vatican Council		2 Editions
1883	The Eternal Priesthood		8 Editions
1880	Holy Ghost the Sanctifier		
1876	Glories of the Sacred Heart		5 Editions
1887	Religio Viatoris		4 Editions
1888	National Education*		

* This is a Sermon. There is also a little volume of articles, with same title, published by Burns and Oates in 1889.

The Cardinal as a Dramatic Critic.

THE CARDINAL AS A DRAMATIC CRITIC.

In no more unexpected character could the Cardinal be shown than in that of a dramatic critic. His feeling against the theatre was deeply rooted, and he had only once in his life sat in the stalls. But when Madame Sara Bernhardt came to London in 1881, and " La Dame aux Camélias " was licensed by a Catholic Lord Chamberlain for the English stage, his indignation, aroused by the mere newspaper reports of the play, found expression in the following article which was published anonymously in the *Weekly Register* at the time. We reproduce here in exact facsimile the MS. of the article: one of those marvellous manuscripts he wrote resting the paper on his knee (as St. John wrote his Gospels in the old masters' pictures), with no ruled lines to guide the pen that made so straight a track across that wilderness of paper.

Though the Comédie Française is over for this season it may visit us again next year. Therefore we think it well that our readers, and especially the heads of Catholic families, should know its true nature. Many have gone to it from fashion; some from frivolity; some from the vanity of being able to talk about it. But most, we hope, from simple unconsciousness of its pernicious character. We will give one sample: and it shall be described not by us, but by the eulogistic critic of a leading journal. The comedy was " La Dame aux Camélias," of Dumas. In passing, we must add that the book from which the comedy is taken is an outrage upon every instinct of modesty in woman and in man. The critic says that: " M. Dumas's apotheosis of a notorious woman of the demi-monde shocked the Parisians themselves," that "the etherealised courtesan" was one of Sarah Bernhardt's " finest and most successful creations," that the play is " unsavoury," " a miry pool," that the heroine is " a woman who scandalised Paris by her luxury, her ostentation, and her extravagance," that she ruined " her titled lovers by the score." The critic admits that " it requires a certain effort of the imagination to conceive such a woman to possess the gentle, affectionate, pure, lofty nature " of M. Dumas's Marguerite. " But this point conceded," the "idyl of love is charming, provided only the spectator can forget the gross, repulsive elements out of which it

The Cardinal as a Dramatic Critic.

is constructed." He then goes on to describe Madame Bernhardt's "creation": its "ineffable sweetness," "fine womanly instinct," etc., "are so true that the audience lose all consciousness of the art by which these results are achieved." Finally, Marguerite is dying of consumption. "Madame Bernhardt plays this scene with *angelic* sweetness which gives it almost the character of a *transfiguration*. We can almost fancy we see the *halo of a Saint* upon her forehead." "She dies in her lover's arms with the words *Ah que je suis bien* upon her lips."

We have given the critic's own words: for any paraphrase of ours would have lessened their moral enormity. And yet the critic all through had a high sense of the grossness of the matter, the iniquity of the author, the evil influence of the actress, and the suspension of moral sense in the audience. Here are four distinct heads of indictment against this abominable offence to all that is chaste in women and honourable in men. But we will not treat of the two first counts. M. Dumas is beyond our reach. The subject matter we leave to the first instincts of all that is pure and noble in human life. The author of "La Dame aux Camélias" belongs to a world that would despise us as much as we abhor it; and in this reciprocal and inextinguishable variance we leave the author and all his works. But of the actress we must say that it is a perilous gift to be able so to play a false and evil part as to draw to falsehood and evil the sympathy and admiration of those who are true and good. If this be not putting "darkness for light and light for darkness," we do not know what it is. The drama is defended as a means of moral education. If so, what defence is to be made for "La Dame aux Camélias," *la virginité de l'âme*, and *la rédemption par l'amour*, with its angelic sweetness, its transfigurations, and its halos of Saints? Human nature is unreal enough already. The intellectual simulation of what we are not is so widespread that few escape it. We are told that

> All the world's a stage
> And all the men and women merely players.
> They have their exits and their entrances.

We are dramatic enough without these elaborate "creations" of transfigured profligacy, and unchastity in halos. We do not desire that our conception of angels should be transferred to courtesans. There is nothing chivalrous in this perversion of the moral life. Vice does not here "lose half its evil by losing all its grossness." It becomes doubly evil because of its intoxicating

Mr. Gladstone's last Tribute.

fascinations. But enough of all this. We hold the Lord Chamberlain gravely responsible for allowing this infamy upon the stage. So high an office demands a little courage; not much : just so much as an independent man always has in incurring, if need be, the enmity of those who put amusement before moral sense. If, however, we cannot acquit the Lord Chamberlain, we must condemn the English fathers and mothers who for any plea or motive exposed themselves and, still more, their children to such subtle and poisonous imaginations. There was a time when the matronly gravity and the maidenly dignity of English women would have resented such a comedy as an insult. We hope, if the like shall come hereafter, some public censure will be branded on it.

MR. GLADSTONE'S LAST TRIBUTE.

The following letter, containing Mr. Gladstone's own and last review of his relations with Cardinal Manning, may be fitly inserted here.

Villa Magali, St. Raphael,
January 25th, 1892.

DEAR MR. ———,

It was indeed very kind of you to write, and to give me such interesting particulars of the deceased Cardinal. The public grief about the Duke of Clarence involved considerations of great width, and seemed to absorb most other matters; but the concurrent death asserted itself, and showed that a deep and extended impression had been made on the general mind—more deep and extended than in the case of Cardinal Newman; and this caused me some surprise. My own relations with Cardinal Manning were very peculiar. First there was a mere acquaintance of two undergraduates at Oxford, which lay wholly on the surface. Then, after an interval, a very close and intimate friendship of somewhere about fifteen years, founded entirely on interests of religion and the Church. Then came his change, which was simultaneous with that of my second and even perhaps yet closer friend, Hope-Scott. Altogether it was the severest blow that ever befell me. In a late letter the Cardinal termed it a quarrel; but in my reply I told him it was not a quarrel, but a death ; and that was the truth. Since then there have been vicissitudes. But I am quite certain that to the last his personal feeling never changed; and I believe also that he kept a promise made in 1851, to remember me before

The Bishop of Newport's Eulogy.

God at the most solemn moments: a promise which I greatly valued. The whole subject is to me at once of extreme interest and of considerable restraint. This I can only illustrate by saying that I was in close relations with Dr. Döllinger (begun in 1845); and between these two there was a sharp antagonism. There is an admirable record of his active friendship with me before 1851 in the series of his own very valuable letters, which he recovered from me at the time; I knew I was parting with a treasure. On Wednesday evening the 13th I received, with surprise as well as pain, at Nimes, a telegram from Sir A. Clark which intimated the crisis and suggested that I should send a message. I did this the same evening, but addressed it to Sir A. Clark; as I did not know whether the suggestion was his own, and felt a scruple about a spontaneous invasion of the death chamber when it may be said the soul is alone with God. I imagine his life to have been as much lifted above the flesh, and as warm with devotion, as many that are justly famous: his reluctance to die may be explained by an intense anxiety to complete unfulfilled service. Repeating my thanks,

I remain, very faithfully yours,

W. E. GLADSTONE.

THE BISHOP OF NEWPORT'S EULOGY.

"*And he spoke to the man that was clothed with linen and said: 'Go in between the wheels that are under the cherubim, and fill thy hands with the coals of fire that are between the cherubim, and pour them out upon the city.*'"—EZECHIEL x. 2.

The Bishop of Newport, taking the above text, said:

An era has closed in the history of Catholicism in England, and a new one has opened. Death is known to be inexorable. The laws of nature, which are the will of God, are fixed and certain, and the end of a human life is as inevitable in its arrival as the beginning of that life is an unchangeable fact. Yet when life has gone on from year to year, when the years have brought no feebleness to the intelligence, no slackness to the will, no lessening of the heart's warmth, hardly a dimness to the eyes, only by slow degrees an observable feebleness to the sense or movement—when such a life is ended, the end is a shock, and there is a feeling as if a great ship, freighted with human

[*] Preached at the London Oratory on the occasion of the funeral of the Cardinal Archbishop, January 21st, 1892.

The Bishop of Newport's Eulogy.

lives, had struck on a rock in mid-ocean. In Westminster, an old man, suddenly, yet not out of Nature's course! At Sandringham, a young man, suddenly too, but at an age when death brings not only grief, but consternation, to those who love the dead! This nation and Empire are mourning at this moment the disappearance of one on whom its hopes have been set. This cruel winter has killed a blossom of its ancient tree, for whom loving hearts were auguring the genial showers of many a spring, the sun of many a ripening summer. It is only those who believe in what is unseen and what is to come who can explain why a father and mother have thus been visited, why a tender heart has been wrung, why a widowed Sovereign has once more been crushed beneath the wreck which death has shaken down upon her head. It is only those who believe in God who can explain how it is that man is so helpless before Nature's blind onset; only those who trust in eternity, who do not despair to see goodness arrested in its tender promise, to see the faculties which nature had given droop and wither like the hand of a dead infant, so lovely in its hope, so pitiful in its cold stillness. The Prince who has been taken from his heart-stricken family, from the wider circle of those who knew and loved him, from the far spread community of a hundred races and tongues which, amid all their differences, looked to him as the heir to the throne which makes them one—has not lived his short life in vain if he has stirred so vast and diverse a brotherhood of peoples with one of those rare and precious emotions which do more than books and philosophy to join men together in love for one another. Providence has given the world a glimpse of him—a brief glimpse—and nothing more. What he might have been we know not. It did not seem presumptuous to see in the future—when some half-a-century had gone by—a gentle, wise, and genial king, honoured by confederated nations, trusted by every class who do the Empire's work, loved by men of every race and colour round the world's circumference. It might have been. In the person of the dead Prince it will never be. "The Lord gave, and the Lord hath taken away." Yet, in that He did give, and that in the taking away He has shown His unspeakable loving kindness—blessed be the name of the Lord! So much could not but be said at a moment when the land is mourning. We turn now to our own loss, and to the sorrow which, a few brief minutes before death visited the Royal House of Britain, fell upon the Catholic Church of England, and the Church throughout the world. After eighty-three years of life, after some forty as a priest of the

THE OBSEQUIES:
A PENCIL SKETCH AT THE ORATORY, JANUARY 21st, 1892.

(*By R. Ponsonby Staples.*)

The Bishop of Newport's Eulogy.

Church of Christ, after six-and-twenty as Bishop of this diocese, Metropolitan of the Province of England, and one of the foremost workers in the greatest capital of the world, there is now to be committed to the earth all that is left to the earth of the Most Reverend and Most Eminent Henry Edward Manning, Cardinal Priest of the Holy Roman Church, Archbishop of Westminster. When we look back, standing by the side of his newly-made grave, to such a career as his, it is difficult to know which feeling is the stronger—whether that of regret that such a head and such a heart are lost to us, or consolation to think of the grand and precious work done in his life, which will now be for all time our inheritance. It seems, on the one hand, as if he might have still gone on. Not three weeks before his death he was writing strongly, lucidly, and warmly, on that difficult problem, how the Catholic body in its poverty can do justice to its devoted and hard-worked teachers. But one week before the end came he was dictating from his bed arrangements for a meeting of the Bishops on this very subject. During these last months—months of rain, of storm, and of darkness—as he sat at his post in the midst of the roar and gloom of this London where his lot was cast, his mind followed with unfailing observation the chronicle of humanity day by day; his door was open to visitors and questioners of every colour and feature, and his word came from him as full of light and distinction almost as in his best days. Such a man can ill be spared. The work is dropped, the pen lies useless, the threads are tangled; the words of counsel will never be completed; the luminous ideas, slowly forming in the atmosphere of thought and prayer, will now remain without form. Who shall take up his work? Who shall fill his place? Who shall lift the lance that is fallen, or wear the armour that he has borne so bravely and so long? When the two prophets of old stood on the river's bank, the younger one—he that was to be left—asked for the "double spirit" of his master. When the fiery chariot parted them, he cried out, "My father, my father; the chariot of Israel and the driver thereof!"—and as he rent his own garments the mantle of Elias fell at his feet. To mourn a master and a leader lost is to prove that we know the worth of those things for which he fought; and the cry which goes up from those who still have to live on and still have to strive is the pledge that they will honour his memory with the best tribute that is possible—the intelligent resolution to carry on the work that will always be linked with his name. There

The Bishop of Newport's Eulogy.

are men who are bidden to fill their hands with the fire which is under the wheels of angelic chariots, and to scatter that fire upon the earth. These men are prophets and apostles, inspired singers, forerunners of Divine visitation. It is not exaggeration, but simple truth, to say that a great priest, with a great office and a great mission, may be, and is, called to gather and to spread heavenly fire. The call need not be limited to great priests, or even to priests at all. Yet, if there is such a thing as the Apostolic succession, the giving of the Holy Ghost, and the mission of teaching men by Christ the Son of God, then have Bishops such a charge as was given in the vision of Ezechiel to him that was clothed in the linen garment. But if pastors, and other men as well, are called, each in his own way, to search for God's fire, and to be the means of kindling it upon the earth, yet not all have the same power to find it, nor have all the same gift to utter it to men. The Divine Spirit, which is continually moving, illuminating, and directing the race of men, has His own ways, His own instruments, His own seasons. What He imparts to the earth is fitly called "fire"; for as fire, so does God's word set aflame the intelligence and the will of man; so does it spread from mind to mind, from heart to heart; so does it from time to time, in vast conflagration, sweep over countries and nations and consume all that cannot stand its searching trial. Sometimes it is a revelation to a people, sometimes the inspired word of a prophet; sometimes it comes in the wind and shock of Pentecost; sometimes in the speech of a Stephen before the Council; sometimes, again, in the preaching of an Apostolic band. These are occasions which are out of Nature's course—when the veil of God's Holy of Holies seems rent in twain, and the Heavenly Father, Who so loves the world, sends forth heavenly fire by the very Seraphim of His presence. But the world is never without men who, without being called into the darkness of Sinai, may with truth be said to be touched by the fire from the altar of Heaven. Such men are moved to see the truth and to give themselves to the expression of it. They are gifted with the power of utterance—a marvellous power, in some respects little short of creation itself—which, out of vague and formless matter, out of the mere hints and flashes of the stream of things as it flows, first forms a living idea, and then gives it an embodiment in language which stamps it upon the intelligence of a generation. It is unnecessary to narrate at length the history and career of the Prince of the Church whose earthly record has now closed for

The Bishop of Newport's Eulogy.

ever. That he was at the age of forty-three a convert from Anglicanism all men know. That he was already a distinguished Churchman of the Anglican Establishment, connected by intellectual ties and bonds of friendship with many of the leaders of the Tractarian Movement, is equally well known. So long as he believed the Church of England to be a part of the Church of Christ, he loved it and honoured it with a filial reverence, and laboured to serve it with fidelity and with conspicuous ability. He was happy during those years. "I loved," he says, "the parish church of my childhood, and the college chapel of my youth, and the little church under a green hillside where the morning and evening prayers, and the music of the English Bible, for seventeen years became a part of my soul. Nothing is more beautiful in the natural order; and if there were no eternal world, I could have made it my home." And the love of those personal friends, so dear to him then, still remained with him in after years, "sweet beyond all words" that he could find to express it. When the sentence of the Crown in the Gorham Case made it clear that in law two absolutely contradictory views on the vital point of the efficacy of Baptism were equally tenable in the Church of England, thirteen members of that Church met together and drew up certain resolutions, which were published in the press. Cardinal Manning spoke, in after times, of the long and earnest discussions which were held in preparing these resolutions, and especially of the "last night, or rather early morning, when at length they were finally agreed to, and the moment to sign them was come." One of those present said to the others—we may easily guess which of them. it was—" If, then, the Church of England shall not clear herself of the Gorham Judgment, we are all, I suppose, prepared to leave her." One spoke in reply—for himself and apparently for some others. Come what might, he said, he had no intention to leave the Church of England. But with Manning it was different. Without passion, without precipitation, in full consciousness of what was due to the sacredness of truth, to public confidence and private friendship, to the truths and duties of past life, he and five others of that conference, feeling that the Anglican Church had confessed she had no power to teach, submitted to the only Church who made any claim to such power. "From that hour," he says, "what was before a conclusion of the intellect became a consciousness of the soul; and an intuition of truth, based upon a Divine certainty, so filled my whole heart and mind, that not only no shadow even of a momentary doubt has ever passed

The Bishop of Newport's Eulogy.

over my conscience or my reason; but a sense of wonder has arisen, how we could so long have failed to perceive a truth which is now self-evident. All I can say is, 'One thing I know, that whereas I was blind, now I see.'" Thus Henry Edward Manning received the Faith; that is, he entered into the possession of what he afterwards called, in many a strong and cogent discourse throughout the length and breadth of this country, "the full light of the Day of Pentecost." I need not recall to those who have heard even one of the innumerable sermons which he delivered in London and elsewhere, how constantly he came back to this. To him there was no more precious gift than the gift of Faith. All his teaching was grounded upon Divine faith. He was never weary of saying that England and Wales had not rejected Faith, but had rather, in the persons of their dumb millions, been robbed of it. His one appeal was to implore them to take it again. "This is what England needs," he used to say; "not wealth, not intellect, not power (though all be good because gifts of God), but the supernatural grace of Faith." What he prayed for, for his countrymen, he cherised and prized for himself. To put faith, religious belief, in front of one's intellectual array, cannot be done without some humiliation of the spirit, some repression of natural prompting, some risk of the contempt of the world. But he knew what was good for himself and for humanity. For men may try to teach the world; but unless their teaching is firmly fixed in God's own word, interpreted by Christ's Church, the teaching of such men will be either discordant from God's Word, and therefore mischievous, or at least inadequate, partial, exaggerated, and incomplete. Among those outside the Catholic Church, in this country during the past half-century, who lifted up their voice in the pulpit, on the platform, and in the Press, and tried to teach the nation, or the world, some have been very great men. Their words have had the power and effect of fire. But the very thunder of their true witnessing has too often made rents and fissures in the temple of truth. This is the Catholic view. We do not expect the world to accept it. But it was Cardinal Manning's. His mind after his conversion was anchored in the harbour. The glory and the danger of adventurous voyages over the seas of theory and fancy unrestrained were not for him. The dangers were real, the glory only imaginary. But he never rested in his efforts to scatter the fire of God. Religion and the spiritual welfare of his flock came first in his heart and in his work. But except politics, which he left alone, is there any province of human interest in which he has not done what is good and lasting? On Education, on the great Labour Question, on the treatment of the Poor, in the promotion of Temperance, he has spoken and written with unceasing devotedness. Every one of these subjects is full of danger in the hands of a man who is not in the possession of the light of Divine faith. It is our consolation, and, I may add, our glory, as children of the Catholic Church, to possess, in the writings of the great Prelate now gone before us, a body of most valuable truth; valuable, because whilst all that he has written is distinguished by his lucidity of thought and the classical penetration of his style, every word is carefully adjusted to God's revelation as interpreted by the Church, and every page bears the impress of a mind which is conscious of Christian and pastoral responsibility. Such words must live; such teachings must spread like the fire of the cherubim. There will be many who will make this very fidelity to supernatural life a reproach; many who will see in it only a proof that he was narrow, retrograde, and inadequate. With such this is not the place nor the moment to contend. It is sufficient, on this occasion, to say that Henry Edward Manning rested his work on the rock of his faith. " Truth comes from Him Who knows what is in man, from Him Who bears in His hand the key of the human intelligence and the human heart. The truth of God . . . alone is the true Key. . . . We see every day that those who try their mutilated religions upon the human intellect and the human heart break the wards and hamper the lock. There is but one key, and that is the key of David. . . . We must choose between two things; we must either believe the Catholic faith, or find a rational and intellectual solution of the unity of truth, and of its adaptation to human nature, and of the existence of the Christian world." I have dwelt upon his religious Faith, because the Cardinal's greatest glory is to have arrested the world's attention by his power of utterance, and at the same time to have ceaselessly reiterated in its hearing the profession of his creed and the psalm of his worship. Many men, and many orders of men, mourn him on this day; and with every one the earnest conviction of his unfailing Catholicism is a powerful element in the kindly thoughts which crowd about his memory. With some—with those of his own Church—it is the subject of praise to God, the motive of regret for his loss, of prayers for his soul. With others—with the many non-Catholics who knew him, who followed his course, who admired his speech and his

The Bishop of Newport's Eulogy.

writing—it must be in a certain degree a mystery; perhaps an annoyance, or a pain. So it must remain. Nothing can alter it now—except that those who think of his Catholicism as a diminution of his fame should, by the grace of God, come to see it in another light. If he prayed and worked for that consummation when he was amongst us, what will he do in that other world, where he is nearer to the throne of Jesus, and more acceptable to Him Who wills to dispense His mercy at the prayer of His holy servants? It is touching to imagine it. "People have come to me with their doubts and anxieties," he has said. Ah! how many? How many men and women, with no faith, or with the vagueness of half-faith, with perplexities of their own, or the weight of others' burdens, with questions on religion, on education, on the rights and duties of working men —seeking for light in the diverse concerns of humanity, from war and peace to the very dwellings and the food of the poor— how many have stood at that door in Westminster, climbed those stone steps, and sat down close to that attenuated form and those kindly eyes, to be helped by his lucid words and cheered by his interest and attention? For a quarter of a century of weeks and days how unfailingly has he been there to bid them welcome, in those rooms which needed nothing to make them genial and inviting except his own presence. No one who ever spoke to him can doubt how, like St. Paul, "he loved everyone in the bowels of Jesus Christ." And even when no visitor was there—during the long hours of his solitude, in the intervals of his prayer, his breviary, and his writing—he turned with wistfulness to the busy life going on round about his watch-tower, longing to help, to lift up, and to save. "With all our faults as a race," he has said, "I recognise in my countrymen noble Christian virtues, exalted characters, beautiful examples of domestic life, and of every personal excellence which can be found where the fulness of grace and truth is not, and much, too, which puts to shame those who are where the fulness of grace and truth abounds." And again: "The Empire of Britain cannot be neutral upon this earth. Its mass is too great to incline its way or that without inclining the world as it sways. For good or evil it must leave its stamp upon the future. Under its shadow must spring up surpassing forms either of life or death. As the Greek and the Latin of old, so the Saxon blood and speech are now spread throughout the earth; a prelude, now as then, of some profound design of God. . . . The earth is girdled with our race, bearing forth with them the institutions,

The Bishop of Newport's Eulogy.

traditions, custom, the nerve, the intelligence, the endurance, the will of England. . . . Not without purposes in Heaven is all this accomplishing. . . . Let us fear nothing but mistrust. We need but Faith, and Faith, too, is a gift of God." Of the bright future foreshadowed, or prayed for, in these words, he saw but little come to pass. Yet not on that account are those words empty. What he himself did for souls and for their needs will never be known till the Judgment Day. There are hundreds, I will be bold to say, listening now to these words, who could speak on this matter far more eloquently than the most eloquent preacher, because they could relate what he did for themselves. And if so many of his friends are still far from his own cherished Faith, what his life failed to accomplish may be accomplished by his death. If the men and women, with genuine hearts, if sometimes with strange and unconventional theories, who came to see him—if they still, perhaps, fail to sympathise with his religion, yet there is that Divine Spirit in Whom he so thoroughly believed; that Spirit Who worketh also outside that Church in which He specially dwells; and the words of the departed may still be fruitful, the seed may still spring up, the bread cast upon the waters may in time be found again. But it is naturally among the brethren of his own household that there is in this hour the deepest mourning for his loss, the truest thanksgiving for his achievements, and the keenest hope from the harvest of his sacrifice and his devotion. And here we venture to think of one who, in his old age and his solitary eminence, can ill afford to lose a friend. Our Holy Father the Pope loved him and leaned upon him. I have heard him speak with his own lips of the wise advice and useful information he received from the Cardinal Archbishop. The Holy See never had a more staunch or more persistent defender. We cannot forget how he wrote upon the "Prerogative of Peter." To him, who fled into the arms of the Catholic Church for safety and security of faith, the Vicar of Christ's Infallibility when addressing the Universal Church on faith or morals was the logical outcome of the Redeemer's promise that against her the gates of hell should never prevail. He read this everywhere in the never-failing Catholic tradition; and as he read it, he laid it before the world in language that was worthy of Tertullian or Cyprian. It has been suggested, even in this hour of his departure, by those who had felt the keenness of his blade, that he exalted the Sovereign Pontiff for the sake of Pontifical honours and rewards. We

The Bishop of Newport's Eulogy.

need not repudiate this unworthy sneer; but one spark of imagination would have enabled an honest writer to place himself within the heart of the illustrious pastor and to see that such a state of feelings was, to him, *impossible*. I will not pause to say how he is mourned by the Bishops of this province, over whom he has presided during so many years. But I cannot forget, and no Bishop that ever knew him will ever forget, that admirable power of rapid thought, perfect form, and lucid utterance, which made every occasion on which he presided at their deliberations one of the rarest intellectual pleasures. But I have a right to turn to the clergy of this diocese. They knew him. It was they whom he loved. They will tell you three things. First, that there is no body of clergy in Europe who have received more earnest, more impressive, and more touching words of instruction than they have been privileged to receive for six-and-twenty years. Next, that no one of them ever went to him without finding in him a father and a friend. And, thirdly, that his personal help, his visits, his marvellous sermons, were regular, unceasing, and kept up to the very last. Well might he say that the dearest wish of his heart was the formation of good and devoted priests. Remember him, O Lord, for this thing! As he prayed and worked to give a worthy and zealous clergy to his flock, so he was himself the chief and most zealous Pastor of all. His name is associated with every pastoral movement, but with none more than the education of the children of the poor. If ever the fire of Heaven was required upon this earth, it is in the Education battle which is raging now in this country and the world over. It was in the very first years of his episcopacy that Cardinal Manning wrote these words: "A Christian child has a right to a Christian education—a Catholic child has a right to a Catholic education." They are the words on which he fought for a quarter of a century. The battle of the children in the unions came first. As far back as 1866 he wrote indignantly on the injustice of forcing Catholic children, whose only crime was poverty, to attend non-Catholic worship and learn non-Catholic catechisms. "We must move every one," he said, "from our gracious Queen —who is the true example of a mother to her children and her subjects—to the least who can contribute a name to a petition." Move he did, and with effect. Partly by means of a change in the law, and partly through his fellow-countrymen's sense of what is right and just, I believe there is not one metropolitan union which now does not send its Catholic children to Catholic institutions. Then came the great and wide question of National Education. To preserve the religion of his own flock he encouraged pastors, built and supported schools, fostered training colleges, and was the warmest friend of teachers. But the world knows that he did more than this. He spoke to the English people. "Is the Christianity of England worth preserving?" This was the question on which he wrote article after article, on which he gave lecture after lecture throughout the country. After the long and patient labours of the Royal Commission, in which he took his full share—with the fullest information, urged by the feeling left upon his mind by inter-communication with the foremost men of the country, he rose to the height of that great occasion, and he formulated his view, that what the country requires is not opposition of conflicting interests, but union of resources—that the School Boards of the country must not be the School Boards that we know too well, but that these must be absorbed and transformed into a grand and general system which shall encourage every Christian teacher's efforts, and neither rob men with a conscience nor deprive any parent of the freedom which is his right. His noble words will not be forgotten. They, too, will live. The struggle is not yet over. Perhaps the hottest and the deadliest hour of the battle is not far off. When it comes he will not be far from us. His powerful words will not lose their power because the voice which uttered them is silent. For we contend, as the Hebrew people under Judas Machabeus, for "our most venerable and holy laws"; and it will not be a vain imagination to see, as was given to the army of Judas to see, even in our midst, one who may fitly be called "the lover of his brethren—he that prayeth much for the people and the holy city"; to feel his presence and to hear him say: "Take this holy sword, a gift from God, wherewith thou shalt overthrow the adversaries of my people" (Machabees xv. 14). My people! That word reminds us that his people were not solely those who venerated him as their spiritual pastor. It was not in virtue of any peculiar mental characteristic that his heart responded to the people's sufferings or the people's aspirations, throughout as wide an area as can be traversed by modern methods of communication. All Christian pastors are the servants of the poor and the labouring man. Above all this is the tradition of great Bishops. No theories of democracy or social rights enter into the motives which force the conscience of a Bishop to labour for those whose

The Bishop of Newport's Eulogy.

condition most resembles that of Christ. But Cardinal Manning had two advantages, which few have in the same degree. He knew the people; and he could speak, both to them and others, in words that none could help attending to. He was infinitely patient in listening and finding out; and he was magnificently convincing in speech when the moment for speech came. Many have seen him with the people; I do not mean in his own house, or in the pulpit of his own church, or formally welcomed by the thousands of his children who loved him; but in some room where chance had brought him—in a shed, perhaps, or a warehouse, or a bare schoolroom, far from the quarters of the rich, on a winter's night, discussing, by the fog-dimmed light, with men who stood and sat around him anyhow—men straight from the street, the workshop, or the river-side, their faces too often whitened with want and sometimes dangerous with passion—discussing, attending, questioning, suggesting, and then finally, with the dignity of his years and his priesthood, holding the assembly silent by the light of his idea and the tones of that earnest voice. The men who labour are not always reasonable; neither are those who employ labour. But Cardinal Manning thought that those who labour have less chance of making themselves heard than those who are better off; and, therefore, like Pope Leo XIII., he spoke for them. The well-known Encyclical "On the Condition of Labour" owes something, beyond all doubt, to the counsels of Cardinal Manning. And there is one sentence in that Letter which, if it was not his in form, most certainly expresses his conviction. "There is a dictate of nature more imperious and more ancient than any bargain between man and man, that the remuneration of the wage-earner must be enough to support him in reasonable and frugal comfort." These words might be inscribed upon the dead Cardinal's grave. We have recalled him, my brethren, in love and mournfulness to our memories in the last hour when we have his remains amongst us. There are some of you who will remind me that I have omitted one picture from this retrospect. It is the picture of one who speaks from a platform—often with humorous words, but always in the deepest earnest—to an audience composed in great part of those children of his, mostly of the race of St. Patrick, whom he loved so deeply. When he thought and spoke of Catholic Ireland—of its fondly treasured Faith, of its piety, which is perennially fed from the fountains of the Sacrament of the Altar and of devotion to the Immaculate Mother —he almost wept. "A narrow channel of sea divides us

The Bishop of Newport's Eulogy.

from a people who speak the same tongue, who are of the same family with us, who are our fellow-countrymen, who are our brothers." It was for them that he instituted the League of the Cross. It was for them that he made some of the very best addresses — so strong, so full of individual character and personal feeling, and withal so affectionate and so fatherly—that he has ever been known to make. He knew well that though drunkenness is a curse, yet there are worse and darker sins. But he also knew that if he could rescue his flock from the sin of excessive drink, situated as they were, he could do nothing better for them. And thousands have blessed his words, his efforts, and that personal asceticism which spread the sacred fire of Temperance throughout this country. Shall the fire die out? Shall the crusade melt away? No; but other hands will take it up, and other voices—not his, yet earnest, too, and persuasive—will bring his words back as the years go on; and, like the bones of the twelve Prophets, his honoured remains will "spring up out of their place" to strengthen pastors and people in the noble cause which he has made his own more than any man, perhaps, of this generation. It is time, now, to let the solemn chant recommence, and to allow the ancient prayers with which the Catholic Church implores rest and refreshment for the souls of its departed children to resume their course. A few more invocations of mercy and the body of a great man will be carried forth, to be laid reverently in the consecrated earth. Not long ago he wrote these words : "Sooner or later—soon at latest, for the longest life is short and fleet in ending—it will go abroad that we are dying. Our turn will come. . . . Will that day come upon us unawares?" He can answer that question now. But it seems to me that we, too, without presumption, can answer it. Many priests know well that touching page in a little book of his in which he describes the death of a "fervent priest." "He has lived by the side of his Divine Master. . . . He has lived among his people, and their feet have worn the threshold of his door. . . . In that dying room, what peace and calm. . . . He fears death, for the Holy Ghost has taught him to know the sanctity of God. . . . But it is a fear that casts out fear, for it is a pledge that the Holy Ghost is in the centre of his soul. . . . Such a death cannot be unprepared. His whole life is a preparation for death." So believe all who knew Henry Edward Manning. And whilst we pray that he may quickly be released from the expiation of the lesser faults of human nature, we think of him

The Bishop of Newport's Eulogy.

as standing, as he will stand, before the Great White Throne, where glows in its centre the fire which the angels minister and which mortal men are privileged to gather and spread. The men and women who have known him in life will disappear one by one. A generation will soon have sprung up who never heard his voice or gazed upon that keen, spiritual, and kindly face. He will be a memory; but a memory bright and lightsome as was his living word and glance. For it is not the stone with its prayer for remembrance that will keep his name before the Church and before his countrymen; not any monument or hatchment, painted picture, or marble bust; but it is the work that he has left; it is the pages in which he has written of the Sacred Heart and of the Holy Spirit, of the priesthood, of the Faith, of the sacredness of childhood, the dignity of the soul, and the nobility of Labour. The fire he found will be bright as long as these conditions of the world last, and these conflicts wage their course. The fiery star has set; but the luminous trail of glory which it has scattered in its passage across the sphere will be there for men to gaze upon, and gazing, to thank God for one who has served so loyally our Heavenly Father and loved with such devotedness the creatures whom the Father loves.

www.ingramcontent.com/pod-product-compliance
Lightning Source LLC
Chambersburg PA
CBHW020309090426
42735CB00009B/1280